CONTENTS

PREFACE

The *Aspects of Psychology* series aims to provide a short and concise, but detailed and highly accessible, account of selected areas of psychological theory and research.

Memory consists of five chapters. Chapter 1 discusses the nature of memory and introduces the Multi-Store model of memory, whilst Chapter 2 looks at some alternatives to this model. Chapter 3 deals with the organisation of information in memory, and Chapter 4 is concerned with theories of forgetting. In Chapter 5, we consider some practical applications of memory research.

For the purposes of revision, we have included detailed summaries of the material presented in each chapter. Instead of a separate glossary, for easy reference the Index contains page numbers in **bold** which refer to definitions and main explanations of particular concepts.

ACKNOWLEDGEMENTS

We would like to thank Dave Mackin, Anna Churchman and Denise Stewart at GreenGate Publishing for their swift and efficient preparation of the text. Thanks also to Greig Aitken at Hodder for all his hard work in coordinating this project (we hope it's the first of many!), and to Tim Gregson-Williams for his usual help and support.

Picture Credits

The publishers would like to thank the following for permission to reproduce photographs and other illustrations in this book:

p86, Fig 5.1 Polygram/Pictorial Press

Every effort has been made to obtain necessary permission with reference to copyright material. The publishers apologise if inadvertently any sources remain unacknowledged and will be glad to make the necessary arrangements at the earliest opportunity.

MEMORY

ASPECTS of PSYCHOLOGY

MEMORY

RICHARD GROSS & ROB MCILVEEN

Hodder & Stoughton
A MEMBER OF THE HODDER HEADLINE GROUP

Dedication

To all students of Psychology: past, present and future

British Library Cataloguing in Publication Data
A catalogue record for this title is available from the British Library

ISBN 0 340 74792 7

First published 1999
Impression number   10 9 8 7 6 5 4 3 2 1
Year   2003 2002 2001 2000 1999

Typeset by GreenGate Publishing Services, Tonbridge, Kent.
Printed and bound in Great Britain for Hodder and Stoughton Educational, a division of
Hodder Headline plc, 338 Euston Road, London NW1 3BH
by Cox and Wyman, Reading, Berks

THE NATURE OF MEMORY AND AN INTRODUCTION TO THE MULTI-STORE MODEL OF MEMORY

Introduction and overview

Reber (1985) identifies three meanings of the word 'memory'. First, it is the mental function of retaining information about events, images, ideas and so on after the original stimuli are no longer present. Second, memory is a hypothesised 'storage system' that holds such information. Third, it is the actual information that has been retained. Whatever meaning we consider, memory clearly plays a central role in all cognitive processes.

Learning is a relatively permanent change in behaviour as a result of experience, and, clearly, without memory we could not benefit from such experience. The uses we have for memory and the amount of information we can store almost defies belief, and it is astonishing to think that an average brain weighing around three pounds can store more information than the world's most advanced supercomputers (Baron, 1989). Yet, memory can also be frustratingly fallible. According to Blakemore (1988):

'Without the capacity to remember and learn, it is difficult to imagine what life would be like, whether we could call it living at all. Without memory we would be servants of the moment, with nothing but our innate reflexes to help us deal with the world. There could be no language, no art, no science, no culture. Civilization itself is the distillation of human memory'.

This chapter examines the nature of memory and considers the *multi-store model of memory*, one of the most influential models attempting to describe memory's structure. It begins by looking at some 'traditions' and 'approaches' to the study of memory, the ways in which memory can be measured, and the concept of memory as 'information processing'.

'Traditions' and 'approaches' to the study of memory

The Ebbinghaus 'tradition'

The systematic, scientific investigation of memory began with Ebbinghaus (1885). To study memory in its 'purest' form, Ebbinghaus invented material which he considered to be meaningless, varied and simple. This consisted of three-letter *nonsense syllables* (a consonant followed by a vowel followed by another consonant, such as XUT and JEQ). Ebbinghaus spent several years using only himself as the subject of his research. He read lists of nonsense syllables out loud, and when he felt that he had recited a list sufficiently to retain it, he tested himself.

If Ebbinghaus achieved two consecutively correct repetitions of a list, he considered it to be learnt. After recording the time taken to learn a list, he then began another one. After specific periods of time, Ebbinghaus would return to a particular list and attempt to memorise it again. The amount he had forgotten could be expressed in terms of the number of attempts (or *trials*) it took him to relearn the list, as a percentage of the number of trials it had originally taken to learn it. If this figure is subtracted from 100 per cent, an indication of the amount 'saved' (*savings score*) is obtained. He found that memory declines sharply at first, but then levels off, a finding which has been subsequently replicated numerous times.

Ebbinghaus carried out many experiments of this sort, and his experimental rigour showed that memory could be scientifically investigated under carefully controlled conditions. He suspected, for example, that memory may not be the same at different times of the day (confirmed by contemporary researchers: see Gross & McIlveen, 1998). In studies conducted between 1883 and 1884, Ebbinghaus *always* tested himself between 1 p.m. and 3 p.m.

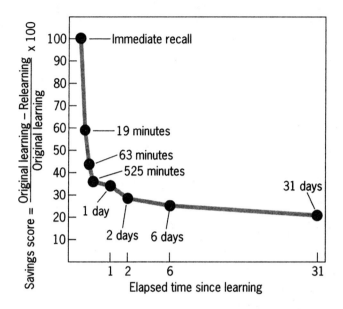

Figure 1.1 *The forgetting curve obtained by Ebbinghaus. The savings score declined very rapidly on the first day, but then levelled off*

The Bartlett 'approach'

The Ebbinghaus 'tradition' (Baddeley, 1976) remains popular with today's memory researchers. Some, though, were critical of Ebbinghaus's methodology. Bartlett (1932) argued that Ebbinghaus excluded 'all that is most central to human memory', and that the study of 'repetition habits' had very little to do with memory in everyday life. If anything, research should examine people's active search for meaning rather than their passive responses to meaningless stimuli presented by an experimenter. Although he accepted that meaningful material is more complex than meaningless material, Bartlett's 'approach' (Baddeley, 1976) argued that it too could be studied experimentally. In one series of experiments, participants were asked to recall an American Indian folktale (*War of the Ghosts*) they had heard after various periods of time. Participants tended to modify the tale in such a way as to make it more consistent with their own frames of reference (Clifford, 1980).

Bartlett proposed that the learning of new things is based on already-existing knowledge (or *schemata*) of the world. He saw both learning and remembering as an *active process* involving 'effort after meaning' (Baddeley, 1976). When existing schemata conflict with new information, distortions occur, as happened with the participants' recall of the folk tale. Whereas Bartlett believed schemata distort the reconstruction of material during its retrieval, Eysenck (1993) thinks it is far more likely that they influence the understanding of material at the time of learning (see Chapter 3).

Baddeley (1976) has noted that memory research has been torn between Ebbinghaus's insistence on simplification (with its danger of trivialisation) and Bartlett's emphasis on memory's complexities (with its danger of being difficult to work with). However, in common with other memory researchers, Baddeley sees the conflict as a healthy one. Neither methodological approach is uniquely correct and both are useful, depending on what aspect of memory is being studied.

The measurement of memory

As noted above, Ebbinghaus's major method of measuring memory involved *relearning*, that is, recording the number of repetitions needed to learn some material compared with the number of repetitions needed to relearn it. Another technique is *recognition*, which involves deciding whether or not a particular piece of information has been encountered before.

In *recall* tasks, participants recall items either in the order in which they were presented (*serial recall*) or in any order they like (*free recall*). One version of serial recall is the *memory-span proce-*

dure. In this, a person is given a number of unrelated digits or letters and then required to immediately repeat them back in the order they were heard. The number of items on the list is successively increased until an error is made. The maximum number of items that can be consistently recalled correctly is a measure of *immediate memory span*.

In *paired-associates* recall tasks, participants are required to learn a list of paired items (such as 'chair' and 'elephant'). When one of the words (e.g. 'chair') is re-presented, the participant must recall the word it was paired with.

Memory as information processing

The concept of information processing derives partly from computer science and its related fields (Baron, 1989). For some researchers, memory can best be understood in terms of the three basic operations involved in the processing of information by modern computers: *registration* (or *encoding*), *storage* and *retrieval*. Advocates of an information-processing approach do not believe that memory operates in *exactly* the same way as a computer. Rather, the approach is a helpful way of conceptualising an extremely complex phenomenon.

Box 1.1 *The three basic information-processing operations involved in memory*

- **Registration (or encoding)** involves the transformation of sensory input (such as a sound or visual image) into a form which allows it to be entered into (or registered in) memory. With a computer, for example, information can only be encoded if it is presented in a format recognisable to the computer.
- **Storage** is the operation of holding or retaining information in memory. Computer data are stored by means of changes in the system's electrical circuitry. With people, the changes occurring in the brain allow information to be stored, though exactly what these changes involve is unclear.
- **Retrieval** is the process by which the information that has been stored is extracted from memory.

Another process is *forgetting*, which is the inability to recall accurately what has been presented. This can occur at the encoding, storage or retrieval stage (see Chapter 4).

Registration can be thought of as a *necessary* condition for storage to take place. However, it is not *sufficient* (since not everything which registers on the senses is stored). Similarly, storage can be seen as a necessary but not sufficient condition for retrieval. Thus, we can only recover information that has been stored, but the fact that something has been stored is no guarantee that it will be remembered on any particular occasion. This suggests a distinction between *availability* (whether or not the information is actually stored) and *accessibility* (whether or not it can be retrieved). This distinction is especially relevant to theories of forgetting (see Chapter 4, page 65).

The nature of memory

James (1890) observed that whilst some information seems to be stored in memory for a lifetime, other information is lost very quickly. He distinguished between two structures or types of memory which he called *primary* and *secondary memory*. These relate to the psychological present and past respectively (Eysenck, 1993). Today, what James called primary memory is referred to as *short-term memory*, whilst secondary memory is referred to as *long-term memory*. To these two types of memory, a third can be added. This is *sensory memory*.

Sensory memory

Sights, sounds and so on are constantly stimulating our senses but not all of this information is important, and an efficient memory system would be one that retained only information which was 'significant' in some way. The function of sensory memory (the *sensory register*) is apparently to retain information for a period of time long enough to enable us to decide whether it is worthy of further processing. The encoding of information in sensory memory is related to the process of *transduction*. This is the transformation of sensory information from the environment into neural impulses that can be processed by our sensory systems and the brain. In the case of the eye, the excitation on the retina lasts for a few tenths of a second after the stimulus has gone.

Mostly, we are unaware of sensory memory. However, if you watch someone wave a lighted cigarette in a darkened room, a streak rather than a series of points will be seen (Woodworth, 1938), indicating the persistence of an image when the stimulus has disappeared. Since humans have several sensory systems, it is likely that a sensory memory exists for all sense modalities. Most research, though, has concentrated on visual and auditory sensory memories.

Visual sensory memory

Much of what is known about visual sensory memory (or *iconic memory*) comes from experiments conducted by Sperling (1960). Sperling used a *tachistoscope* to flash visual displays to participants for very brief periods of time (around 50 to 100 milliseconds). In the *whole-report procedure*, participants had to identify as many of nine letters (arranged in three rows of three) as they could. Participants could typically identify a maximum of four or five correctly. They claimed, however, that they could actually remember more than that, but that after naming four or five, the image of them had faded completely.

To test these claims, Sperling used the *partial-report procedure*. In this, the three rows of three letters were again presented tachistoscopically, but were immediately followed by a high-, medium- or low-pitched tone. The tone was the signal for the participant to recall the top, middle or bottom row of letters respectively. When the tone *preceded* the presentation of the visual display, recall was (not unexpectedly) almost faultless. When the tone *followed* the display's presentation, recall was almost as good, even though participants had to retrieve the information from the sensory register. Sperling concluded that the capacity of sensory memory is large, and may even be large enough to hold brief representations of virtually everything that impinges on the visual sensory system (Reeves & Sperling, 1986).

In other experiments, Sperling delayed sounding the tone after the visual display had been presented. With a half a second delay, recall was only 63 per cent accurate, and after one second very little was recalled, suggesting that visual sensory memory is like a 'rapidly decaying mental photograph' (Hassett & White, 1989). Because information decays so rapidly, then, it is hardly surprising that participants in the whole-report procedure were unable to recall more items than they did.

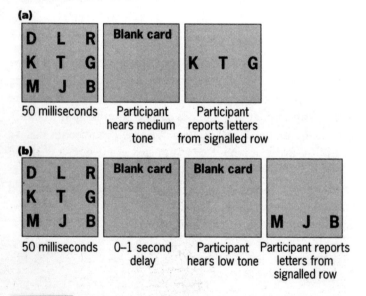

Figure 1.2 *(a) shows Sperling's partial-report method, and (b) shows the partial-report method with a delay*

Auditory sensory memory

Auditory sensory memory (*echoic memory*, or what Morton, 1970, calls the *pre-categorical acoustic store*) is very similar, if not identical to Broadbent's *sensory buffer store* (see Gross &

McIlveen, 1998). Echoic memory enables us to hear a sound after it has stopped. Since we cannot identify a word until we have heard all the sounds that make it up, echoic memory is necessary to hold a representation of an initial sound until the whole word has been heard. Only then can the sound be put into context (Baddeley, 1995). Probably for this reason, echoic memory persists for longer than iconic memory. It can last as long as ten seconds, depending on the method of measurement used (Cowan, 1984), but an upper limit of around four seconds is more realistic (Darwin *et al.*, 1972).

As noted earlier, sensory registration is a *necessary* but not sufficient condition for information storage. Something must be done with the information very quickly if the material is to be passed on for further processing (see Box 1.2). Also, it is likely that there is a sensory memory for all sense modalities (sensory memory is *modality specific*).

Box 1.2 *The 'attentional gate'*

Reeves & Sperling (1986) asked participants to watch a stream of letters appearing in their left visual field. Participants were instructed to shift their attention to their right visual field whenever a target (the letters C, U or a square) appeared in their left visual field. A stream of numbers was already being presented in the right visual field, and participants had to report the first four numbers they saw.

The time between the occurrence of a target and the reporting of a number was taken as a measure of how quickly attention could be shifted, and the researchers assumed that this interval would indicate how long an 'attentional gate' between sensory memory and short-term memory (STM) remained open.

The gate remained open for around 0.4 seconds, and participants could not report the numbers they saw in the correct order, even though they thought they could, suggesting a loss of information during the transfer from sensory memory to STM.

Short-term memory

Probably less than one-hundredth of all the sensory information that impinges every second on the human senses reaches consciousness, and of this only about five per cent achieves anything like stable storage (Lloyd *et al.*, 1984). Clearly, if we possessed only sensory memory, our capacity for retaining information would be extremely limited. Information that has not been lost from the sensory register is passed on to a second storage system called *short-term memory* (STM).

The capacity of STM

Miller (1956) showed that most people could store only about seven *independent* items (numbers, letters, words). He used the word *chunk* to refer to a discrete piece of information. So, when people attempt to remember an *unrelated* string of letters, each constitutes one chunk of information. However, STM's capacity could be enlarged if separate pieces of information were *combined* into a larger piece of information.

For example, the sequence 246813579 can be 'chunked' by applying a rule concerning odd and even numbers. The amount that can be held in STM, then, depends on the *rules* which are used to organise the information. For Miller, the capacity of STM is seven plus or minus two chunks rather than individual pieces of information.

Box 1.3 *Miller and the concept of 'chunking'*

Miller argues that chunking is a linguistic recoding which is 'the very lifeblood of the thought process'. In his view, chunking is not a surprising phenomenon given how lexical information is normally processed. Thus, our capacity to read and understand is largely based on the chunking of letters into words, words into phrases, and phrases into sentences. So, STM's ability to deal with a vast amount of information is facilitated by the chunking of information. However, we cannot do this until certain information in *long-term memory* (LTM) has been activated and a match made between incoming information and its representation in LTM.

Miller & Selfridge (1950) gave participants 'sentences' of varying lengths which approximated true English (to different degrees), and asked them to recall the words in their correct order. The closer a 'sentence' approximated true English, the better immediate recall of it was. This suggests that knowledge of semantic and grammatical structure (presumably stored in LTM) is used to facilitate recall from STM.

In a conceptually similar study, Bower & Springston (1970) presented some participants with a letter sequence in which the letters were presented in a way that formed a well-known group (e.g. fbi, phd, twa, ibm). Others were presented with the same letters but in a way that did not form a well-known group (e.g. fb, iph, dtw, aib, m). The former recalled many more letters than the latter, the material to the former being clustered in acronyms familiar to most American college students. In effect, the pause after 'fbi' and so on allowed participants to 'look up' the material in their mental lexicon and so encode the letters in one chunk.

Coding in STM

Conrad (1964) presented participants with a list of six consonants (such as BKSJLR), each of which was seen for about three-quarters of a second. Participants were then instructed to write down what they had seen. The errors they made tended to be linked to a letter's *sound*. For example, there were 62 instances of B being mistaken for P, 83 instances of V being mistaken for P, but only two instances of S being mistaken for P. These *acoustic confusion errors* suggested to Conrad that STM must code information according to its sound. When information is presented visually, it must somehow be *transformed* into its acoustic code.

However, STM also codes information in other ways. For example, Shulman (1970) visually presented participants with lists of ten words. They were then tested for their recognition of them using a visually presented 'probe word'. The probe word was a homonym of one of the words on the list (such as 'bawl' instead of 'ball'), a synonym (such as 'talk' instead of 'speak'), or was identical to it. Shulman found that *homonym* and synonym probes produced similar error rates, implying that some *semantic coding* (or coding for meaning) had taken place in STM, since if an error was made on a synonym probe, some matching for meaning must have taken place. Other research indicates that visual images (such as abstract pictures, which would be hard to store in the form of an acoustic code) can be maintained in STM, if only briefly.

The duration of STM

A way of studying 'pure' STM was devised by Brown (1958) and Peterson & Peterson (1959), and is called the Brown–Peterson technique. By repeating something that has to be remembered (*maintenance rehearsal*), information can be held in STM almost indefinitely.

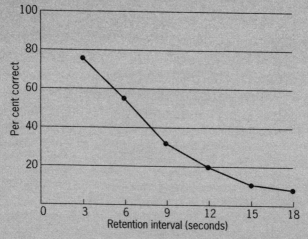

Box 1.4   *The Brown–Peterson technique*

The *Brown–Peterson technique* involves participants hearing various trigrams (such as XPJ). Immediately afterwards, they are instructed to recall what they heard or to count backwards in threes from some specified number for a pre-determined period of time (the *retention interval*). The function of this *distractor* task is to prevent rehearsal. At the end of the time period, the trigram must be recalled.

Figure 1.3   *The data reported by Peterson and Peterson in their experiment on the duration of STM*

Peterson and Peterson found that the average percentage of correctly recalled trigrams was high with short delays, but decreased as the delay interval lengthened, dropping to a mere six per cent after only 18 seconds. In the absence of rehearsal, then, STM's duration is very short, and it can be made even shorter if a more difficult distractor task is used (Reitman, 1974).

Long-term memory

Long-term memory (LTM) has been conceptualised as a vast storehouse of information in which memories are stored in a relatively permanent way. Exactly how much information can be stored in LTM is not known, but most psychologists agree that there is no evidence for any limit to LTM's capacity. In contrast with STM, then, the *capacity* of LTM is far greater and its duration is also considerably longer.

With verbal material, *coding* in LTM appears to be primarily according to its *meaning* (semantic coding). For example, Baddeley (1966) presented participants with words which were acoustically similar (such as 'mad', 'man' and 'mat'), semantically similar ('big', 'broad' and 'long'), acoustically dissimilar ('foul', 'old' and 'deep'), or semantically dissimilar ('pen', 'day' and 'ring'). When recall from STM was tested, acoustically similar words were recalled less well than acoustically dissimilar words (supporting the claim that acoustic coding occurs in STM). Semantically similar words were significantly less well recalled than semantically dissimilar words, although this difference was very small (64 per cent compared with 71 per cent), a finding which suggests that whilst some semantic coding occurs in STM, it is not the dominant method.

When an equivalent study was conducted on LTM, semantically similar material impaired long-term recall, but acoustically similar material had no effect. Such findings do *not* imply that LTM only codes material semantically (Baddeley, 1976). The fact that we can conjure up the image of a place we visited on holiday indicates that at least some information is stored or coded in *visual* form. Also, some types of information are coded *acoustically* in LTM (such as songs). Smells and tastes are also stored in LTM, suggesting that as well as being large and long-lasting, it is also a very flexible system (see Chapter 2).

The multi-store model

Atkinson & Shiffrin's (1968, 1971) multi-store model of memory (sometimes called the *dual-memory model* because of its emphasis on STM and LTM) was an attempt to explain the flow of information from one system to another. The model sees sensory memory, STM and LTM as *permanent structural components* of the memory system and intrinsic features of the human information-processing system (see Figure 1.4). In addition to these structural components, the memory system comprises relatively transient *control processes*.

One important transient process is *rehearsal,* which has two functions. First, it acts as a buffer between sensory memory and LTM by maintaining incoming information within STM. Second, it enables information to be transferred to LTM. Although Atkinson and Shiffrin saw rehearsal as the most common method of transfer, they accepted that there were other ways in which material could be transferred. Indeed, they suggested that it was even possible for information to bypass STM and enter LTM directly from the sensory register, a point which some of their critics tend to ignore (see below).

Two lines of evidence supporting Atkinson and Shiffrin's view that STM and LTM may be considered to be separate and distinct storage systems come from *experimental studies of STM and LTM* and *clinical studies of amnesics.*

Experimental studies of STM and LTM

Murdock (1962) presented participants with a list of words at a rate of about one per second. They were required to free-recall as many of these as they could. The words were not equally likely to be recalled, and those at the beginning and the end of the list were much more likely to be recalled than those in the middle. Murdock called this the *serial position effect*.

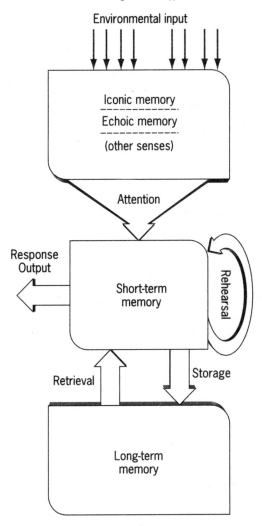

Figure 1.4 *The multi-store/dual-memory model of memory proposed by Atkinson and Shiffrin*

The superior recall of the items that appeared at the beginning of the list is called the *primacy effect*, whilst the superior recall of those at the end is called the *recency effect*. The primacy effect occurs because the items at the beginning of the list have presumably been rehearsed and transferred to LTM from where they are recalled. To test the idea that items are transferred through rehearsal, Rundus & Atkinson (1970) asked participants performing a Murdock-type task to rehearse out loud the list they were presented with. Tape recordings indicated that words from the beginning of the list were more likely to be rehearsed than later ones. The recency effect can be explained in terms of items currently held in STM being recalled from that system. Because STM's capacity is limited and can only hold items for a brief period of time, words in the middle of the list are thought to be either lost from the system completely or otherwise unavailable for recall.

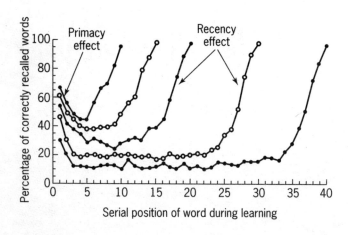

Figure 1.5   *Serial position curves for word lists of different lengths*

In a variation of Murdock's study, Glanzer & Cunitz (1966) showed that delaying recall of a list of words for 30 seconds and preventing rehearsal (by using Peterson and Peterson's counting task) resulted in the recency effect disappearing, but the primacy effect remaining (see Figure 1.6). Presumably, the earlier words had been transferred to LTM (from where they were recalled), whilst the most recent words were 'vulnerable' to the counting task (Eysenck, 1993). Other research (e.g. Murdock & Walker, 1969) has shown that under certain conditions, the recency effect can be left intact, but the primacy effect massively depressed.

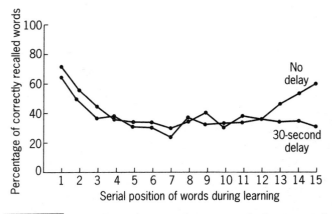

Figure 1.6 *Data from Glanzer and Cunitz's study showing serial position curves after no delay and a delay of 30 seconds*

Clinical studies of amnesics

Amnesics are people who suffer memory loss, usually as a result of brain damage. If STM and LTM are distinct and separate storage systems, then certain types of damage affecting only one of the systems should leave the other intact, which would be reflected in the person's ability to remember. In *Korsakoff's syndrome*, found in chronic alcoholics, STM appears to be intact, it is possible to carry on a normal conversation with them, and they are capable of reading a newspaper. However, the transfer of information to LTM is seriously impaired, and they may have no memory of a conversation taking place or of a paper having been read.

Shallice & Warrington (1970) reported the case of K.F., a man who had suffered brain damage as a result of a motorbike accident. His STM was severely impaired, and he could often recall no more than one or two digits on a digit span test. However, his LTM for events occurring after the accident was normal. This also supports the view that STM and LTM are separate and distinct, and suggests that information can find its way into LTM even if STM is severely impaired (see page 14).

Other research, using PET and MRI scanning devices, suggests the existence of multiple memory systems. Periani *et al.* (1993), for example, reported differential changes in brain structure metabolism according to the type of amnesia a person was experiencing, with the hippocampus, thalamus and cingulate gyrus being important structures (see Gross & McIlveen, 1998).

Box 1.5 *A case of amnesia caused by hippocampal damage*

In March 1985, Clive Wearing, former chorus master of the London Sinfonietta, suffered a brain infection caused by the herpes simplex (cold sore) virus. As well as damaging parts of his cortex, the virus destroyed his hippocampus. The consequence of this is that Wearing appears to be unable to transfer new information from STM to LTM, and as a result lives in a 'snapshot' of time constantly believing that he has just awoken from years of unconsciousness. Thus, he reacts to people as if they had been parted for years, even though those people might have paid him a visit minutes earlier.

Wearing can still speak and walk, as well as play the organ and conduct, and his musical ability is remarkably well preserved. He can learn some new skills, and these appear to be stored in LTM. However, whenever he is asked to perform the skill, he reacts as though he has never attempted to learn it before. His memory of his early life is patchy, and his ability to recall details of his life extremely poor.

When shown pictures of Cambridge, where he had studied, he recognised King's College chapel (the most well known and distinctive building in Cambridge) but did not recognise his own college. He could not remember who wrote *Romeo and Juliet*, and identified the Queen and the Duke of Edinburgh as singers he had known from a Catholic church.

Wearing's lack of conscious recollection is, in his own words, 'Hell on earth – it's like being dead – all the bloody time'.

(Adapted from Blakemore, 1988; Baddeley, 1990)

Other cases involving effects similar to those seen in Clive Wearing include three children who had suffered hippocampal damage early in life. All were unable to remember everyday events, such as where their belongings were located or what day it was. Incredibly, though, they all attended mainstream schools and learned to read and write with average competency (Highfield, 1997).

Some challenges to the multi-store model

Despite the continuing influence of the multi-store model in memory research, it has been argued that there is no real need to make a distinction between the various storage systems and that it is far more profitable to view them as being different phases of a continuous process. Moreover, Atkinson and Shiffrin's 'compartmentalisation' of memory into units from which information flows has also been challenged.

Box 1.6   *The two-way flow of information between STM and LTM*

Certainly, studies suggest that it is highly unlikely that STM contains only *new* information. What seems more likely is that information is retrieved from LTM for use in STM. For example, the string of numbers 18561939 may appear to be independent. However, they can be 'chunked' into one unit according to the rule 'the years in which Sigmund Freud was born and died'. If we can impose meaning on a string of digits, we must have learned this meaning *previously*, the previously learned rule presumably being stored in LTM. In this case, information has flowed not only from STM to LTM but also in the opposite direction.

A vivid example of this comes from studies of people who are experts in some particular domain. De Groot (1966), for example, showed that expert chess players had a phenomenal STM for the position of chess pieces on a board *provided* they were organised according to the rules of chess. When the pieces were randomly arranged, experts' recall was no better than that of non-chess players. With chess experts, information from LTM about the rules of chess were used to aid recall from STM.

Other researchers have challenged the role of rehearsal in the multi-store model. Craik & Watkins (1973) asked participants to remember only certain 'critical' words (those beginning with a particular letter) from lists presented either rapidly or slowly. The position of the critical words relative to the others determined the amount of time a particular word spent in STM and the number of potential rehearsals it could receive. Retention over long periods was unrelated to either the amount of time a word had spent in STM or the number of explicit or implicit rehearsals.

Based on this and other findings (e.g., Glanzer & Meinzer, 1967), Craik and Watkins have distinguished between *maintenance rehearsal* (see page 25), in which material is rehearsed in the form in which it was presented ('rote'), and *elaborative rehearsal* (or *elaboration of encoding*) which *elaborates* the material in some way (such as by giving it a meaning or linking it with pre-existing knowledge). It is the *kind* of rehearsal or processing that is important rather than the *amount* of rehearsal (Craik & Lockhart, 1972). The evidence for this distinction is considered in Chapter 2.

Conclusions

This chapter has discussed some of the findings relating to the nature of memory and considered the multi-store model as a way of conceptualising how various storage systems are linked. Although influential, and supported by evidence, the multi-store model has been the subject of criticism and alternatives to it have been advanced.

Summary

- Memory was first studied systematically by Ebbinghaus, using **nonsense syllables** to study it in its 'purest' form, and himself as the sole subject. He found that memory declines rapidly at first before levelling off, a finding subsequently replicated many times.

- Bartlett criticised Ebbinghaus's approach for being largely irrelevant to memory in everyday life. Research should examine people's active search for meaning rather than passive 'repetition habits'. Learning new material is based on already-existing **schemata**.

- Ebbinghaus assessed memory using **relearning**. Other methods include **recognition**, **serial** or **free recall** and **paired associates** recall tasks.

- The **information-processing approach** sees registration (**encoding**) as necessary for **storage**, the retention of the information in memory. Not everything that is registered on the senses is stored, and not everything that is stored can be **retrieved**.

- James distinguished between **primary** (referred to today as **short-term**) and **secondary** (**long-term**) **memory**, relating to the psychological **present** and **past** respectively.

- **Sensory memory** (or the **sensory register**) retains information just long enough for us to decide whether or not it is worthy of further processing. The image of a stimulus must persist for a brief time after the stimulus has been removed, otherwise we would be unable to respond to it. Sensory memory is **modality-specific** and research has concentrated on the visual (**iconic**) and auditory (**echoic**) modalities.

- Sperling's **whole-report** and **partial-report procedures** suggest that sensory memory has a large capacity and that information decays very rapidly from it.

- **Echoic memory** (the **pre-categorical acoustic store**) enables us to hear a sound after it has stopped. This is necessary for identifying spoken words.

- Only a fraction of all the information that reaches the senses at any one time is actually stored. If memory were limited to sensory memory, our capacity for retaining information would be extremely restricted.

- According to Miller, STM's capacity is seven plus or minus two **chunks** of information. If unrelated or independent items of information are **combined** (**'chunked'**), STM's capacity can be increased.

- **Acoustic confusion errors** indicate that STM **codes** information **acoustically**. There is also evidence of **semantic coding**, and visual images can be briefly maintained in STM.

- The **Brown–Peterson technique** shows that by using a **distractor** task to prevent rehearsal, almost no information is recalled after an 18-second **retention interval**.

- LTM's **capacity** is apparently limitless. Its **duration** is also considerably longer than STM's, with information probably being stored permanently. The **coding** of verbal material in LTM is primarily **semantic**, but other information is coded **visually** and **acoustically**. LTM is a very flexible system.

- According to Atkinson and Shiffrin's **multi-store/dual-memory model**, sensory memory, STM and LTM are **permanent structural components** of the memory system, with STM and LTM being distinct storage systems. **Rehearsal** is a transient **control process**.

- Rehearsal acts as a buffer between sensory memory and LTM and also aids the transfer of information to LTM. But information can enter LTM directly from the sensory register.

- According to Murdock's **serial position effect**, free recall of a list of words produces better recall at the **beginning** and **end** of the list (the **primacy** and **recency effect** respectively). The primacy effect is taken to reflect recall from LTM, whilst the recency effect reflects recall from STM.

- **Clinical studies of amnesics** also support the STM/LTM distinction. In people with **Korsakoff's amnesia**, STM appears to be intact, but the transfer of information to LTM is seriously impaired.

- Studies using PET and MRI also support the idea of multiple memory systems, with the hippocampus, thalamus and cingulate gyrus all apparently playing important roles.

- Although the multi-store model continues to be influential, it may be unnecessary to distinguish between the various storage systems. Rather than seeing STM as containing only **new** information, it is likely that information is retrieved from LTM for use in STM, as in chunking.

- The kind of rehearsal proposed by the multi-store model is what Craik and Watkins call **maintenance rehearsal**, which they distinguish from **elaborative rehearsal** (**elaboration of encoding**). What matters is the **kind** of rehearsal or processing, rather than the amount.

SOME ALTERNATIVES TO THE MULTI-STORE MODEL OF MEMORY

Introduction and overview

2

As noted in Chapter 1, the multi-store model of memory has attracted both support and criticism. This chapter considers three major efforts to revise Atkinson and Shiffrin's model. Craik and Lockhart argue against its claim that memory can be 'compartmentalised', Baddeley reconceptualises the nature of STM, and Tulving challenges the claim that LTM is unitary. Whilst all these alternatives are critical of the multi-store model, none is an outright rejection of it. Rather, they all see the multi-store model as an oversimplified account of our highly complex memory.

The levels-of-processing model

Although Craik & Lockhart (1972) accepted that the multi-store model accommodated research findings reasonably well, they argued that there was also evidence directly contradicting it. As noted in Chapter 1 (see page 20), their distinction between maintenance and elaborative rehearsal allowed them to argue that the amount of rehearsal *per se* was less important in determining the transfer of information than the *type* of rehearsal (as supported by Craik & Watkins', 1973, study).

It was also seen that the multi-store model distinguishes between the *structural components of memory* (sensory memory, STM and LTM) and *control processes* (such as rehearsal and coding), with the latter being tied to the former. It emphasises the sequence of processing stages that information goes through as it passes from one structural component to another. Craik and Lockhart, however, began with the hypothesised processes and then formulated a memory system (the structural components) in terms of these operations.

They saw memory as a by-product of perceptual analysis. A crucial concept is the *central processor*, capable of analysing data on various levels and of finite capacity and therefore incapable of dealing with all aspects of a stimulus. The surface features of a stimulus (such as whether a word is in lower or upper case letters) are analysed superficially (processed at a *shallow level*). The semantic features (such as a word's meaning) are analysed more extensively (processed at a *deep level*). Lying between these two extremes, a verbal stimulus can also be analysed according to its sound (processed at a *phonemic* or *phonetic* level).

The level used depends on both the nature of the stimulus and the processing time available. The more deeply information is processed, the more likely it is to be retained.

Box 2.1 *Craik & Tulving's (1975) experiment*

Craik & Tulving (1975) presented participants with a list of words via a tachistoscope. Following each word, participants were asked one of four questions to which they had to respond 'yes' or 'no'. The four questions were:

1 Is the word (e.g. TABLE/table) in capital letters?
2 Does the word (e.g. hate/chicken) rhyme with 'wait'?
3 Is the word (e.g. cheese/steel) a type of food?
4 Would the word (e.g. ball/rain) fit in the sentence 'He kicked the ... into the tree'?

Question (1) corresponds to structural processing, (2) to phonetic processing, and (3) and (4) to semantic processing. Later, participants were unexpectedly given a test in which the words they had seen appeared amongst words they had not seen. The task was to identify which words had been presented earlier. There was significantly better recognition of words that had been processed at the deepest (semantic) level. Additionally, recognition was superior when the answer to the question was 'yes' rather than 'no'.

It has also been found that *elaboration* (the *amount* of processing of a particular kind at a particular level) is important in determining whether material is stored or not. For example, Craik &

Tulving (1975) asked participants to decide if a particular word would be appropriate in simple sentences such as 'She cooked the …' or complex sentences such as 'The great bird swooped down and carried off the struggling …'. When participants were later given a *cued recall* test, in which the original sentences were again presented but without the particular words, recall was much better for those compatible with the complex sentences. Since the same depth of (semantic) processing occurred in both cases, some additional factor (elaboration) must also be involved.

Bransford *et al.* (1979) showed that the *nature* of the elaboration is more important than the amount of elaboration. Minimally elaborated sentences such as 'A mosquito is like a doctor because they both draw blood' were better remembered than multiply elaborated similies like 'A mosquito is like a racoon because they both have hands, legs and jaws'. Possibly, this is because material which is *distinctive* in some way is more likely to be remembered. This is another way of conceptualising 'depth' – it may be the non-distinctiveness of shallow encodings (as opposed to their shallowness *per se*) which leads to their poor retention (Eysenck & Keane, 1995).

It is often difficult to choose between level of processing, elaboration and distinctiveness because they can occur together (Eysenck, 1993). Retention cannot be predicted solely on the basis of processing level because more elaborate or distinctive semantic encodings are usually better remembered than non-elaborate or non-distinctive ones. Thus, Eysenck & Eysenck (1980) found that a shallow level of processing could result in remembering that was almost as good as a deep level, as long as it was also distinctive. Quite possibly, all three make separate contributions to remembering, but distinctiveness, which relates to the nature of processing and takes account of relationships between encodings, is probably more important than elaboration, which is only a measure of the amount of processing (Eysenck, 1986).

Evaluation of the levels-of-processing model

The model was proposed as a new way of interpreting existing data and to provide a conceptual framework for memory research. It is generally accepted that it contains some truth, and that perception, attention and memory are interdependent. Prior to 1972, few studies had compared the effects on memory of different kinds of processing, because it was implicitly assumed that any particular stimulus would typically be processed in a very similar way by all participants on all occasions. For Parkin (1987), the model has led to general acceptance of the idea that *processing strategies* may provide at least the basis for understanding memory.

However, many researchers see the model as rather simplistic and predominantly descriptive rather than explanatory (Eysenck & Keane, 1995). For example, it fails to address the question of *why* deeper processing leads to better recall. Another problem concerns the difficulty of defining or measuring depth *independently* of a person's actual retention score. So, if 'depth' is defined as 'the number of words remembered', and 'the number of words remembered' is taken as a measure of 'depth', the model's logic is *circular*. Although attempts have been made to provide an independent measure of depth (e.g. Hyde & Jenkins, 1973), there is no *generally accepted* way of independently assessing depth. This 'places major limits on the power of the levels-of-processing approach' (Baddeley, 1990).

Finally, some studies have directly contradicted the model. For example, Morris (1977) showed that rhyming recognition tests produce better recall when they are processed at the 'shallow' than the 'deep' level. Apparently, the *relevance* of the processing is influential. If material is usually processed at a shallow level, recall is better at that level. According to Parkin (1993), the different instructions participants are given vary in terms of the extent to which they require them to treat the stimulus as a word (compare, for example, 'Is a "tiger" a mammal?' with 'Does "tiger" have two syllables?'), yet retention tests *always* require participants to remember words. Since semantic tasks, by definition, require attention to be paid to stimuli as words, their superior retention could reflect the bias of the retention test towards the type of information being encoded.

Reconceptualising short-term memory: the working-memory model

Baddeley & Hitch (1974) criticised the multi-store model's concept of a *unitary* STM. Whilst not rejecting the multi-store model's view of STM as rehearsing incoming information for transfer to LTM, they argued that it was much more complex and versatile than a mere 'stopping-off station' for information. For example, information can flow from LTM to STM as well as in the other direction. Whenever we begin a sentence, we think about what we are going to say (which must be based on information stored in LTM) as well as what we have just said.

Baddeley and Hitch's concept of STM as a *working-memory store* emphasises that it is an active store used to hold information which is being manipulated. For Cohen (1990), working memory is:

'the focus of consciousness – it holds the information you are consciously thinking about now'.

The original model has been modified and elaborated by Baddeley and his colleagues (e.g. Baddeley, 1981, 1986; Salame & Baddeley, 1982). In its present form, it consists of a system in 'overall charge' (the *central executive*) and a number of sub-systems or *slave systems* whose activities are directed by the central executive. These are the *articulatory loop*, *visuo-spatial scratch pad* (or *sketch pad*), and *primary acoustic store*.

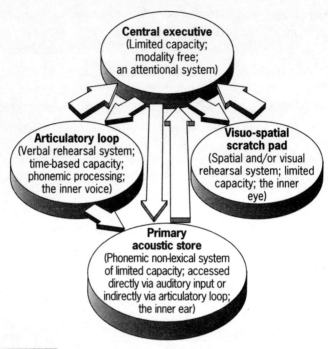

Figure 2.1   *The working-memory model*

The central executive

This is used whenever we deal with a task which makes cognitive demands. Although capacity limited, it is very flexible and can process information in any sense modality (it is *modality free*) in various ways. The central executive approximates to a *pure attentional system* (Baddeley, 1981).

The articulatory (or phonological) loop

This can be regarded as a verbal rehearsal loop used when, for example, we try to remember a telephone number for a few seconds by saying it to ourselves. It is also used to hold words we are preparing to speak aloud. Because it uses an *articulatory/phonological code*, in which information is represented as it would be spoken, it has been called the *inner voice*.

The visuo-spatial scratch pad

This can also rehearse information, but deals with visual and/or spatial information as, for example, when we drive along a familiar road, approach a bend, and think about the road's spatial layout beyond the bend (Eysenck, 1986: see Figure 2.2). Because it uses a *visual code*, representing information in the form of its visual features such as size, shape and colour, it has been called the *inner eye*. Baddeley (1986) describes the visuo-spatial scratch pad as:

'a system especially well adapted to the storage of spatial information, much as a pad of paper might be used by someone trying, for example, to work out a geometric puzzle'.

Figure 2.2 *The visuo-spatial scratch pad is where we store information about familiar roads, so we know what is round the bend*

The primary acoustic store

This receives auditory input directly, but visual input can only enter it indirectly, after it has been processed by the articulatory loop and *converted* to a phonological form. Because it uses an *acoustic/phonemic code*, representing information in the form of auditory features such as pitch and loudness, it is called the *inner ear*.

Box 2.2   *Working memory in action*

One way of understanding how working memory operates can be gained from trying to determine the number of windows you have in your house (Baddeley, 1995). Most of us attempt to do this by forming a visual image and then either 'looking' at the house from the outside or taking a 'mental journey' through its various rooms. To set up and manipulate the image, we need the visuo-spatial scratch pad, and to sub-vocally count the number of windows we need the articulatory loop. The whole operation is organised and run by the central executive.

Research into working memory has often used the *concurrent* or *interference-* (or *dual-*) *task method* (similar to studies on divided attention: see Gross & McIlveen, 1998). Assuming that each slave system's capacity is limited, then with two tasks making use of the same component(s), performance on one or both should be worse when they are performed together than when they are performed separately (Baddeley *et al.*, 1975). If two tasks require different slave systems, it should be possible to perform them as well together as separately. Some researchers have used *articulatory suppression*, in which the participant rapidly repeats out loud something meaningless (such as 'hi-ya' or 'the'). This uses up the articulatory loop's resources, so it cannot be used for anything else. If articulatory suppression produces poorer performance on another task being performed simultaneously, then we can infer that this task also uses the articulatory loop (Eysenck & Keane, 1995).

An evaluation of the working memory model

It is generally accepted that STM is better seen as a number of relatively independent processing mechanisms than as the multi-store model's single unitary store. It is also generally accepted that attentional processes and STM are part of the *same* system, mainly because they are probably used together much of the time in everyday life. The idea that any one component of working memory (such as the articulatory loop) may be involved in the performance of apparently very different tasks (such as memory span, mental arithmetic, verbal reasoning and reading) is also a valuable insight. The working-memory model also has practical applications which extend beyond its theoretical importance (Gilhooly, 1996).

Box 2.3 *Working memory and learning to read*

The articulatory loop is 'not just a way of linking together a number of laboratory phenomena' (Baddeley, 1990). Rather it (or some similar system) plays an important part in learning to read. One of the most striking features of children with specific problems in learning to read (despite being of normal intelligence and having a supportive family background) is that they have an impaired memory span (Gathercole & Baddeley, 1990). They also tend to do rather poorly on tasks which do not directly test memory, such as judging whether words rhyme. Such children might experience some form of phonological deficit (detectable before the child has even begun to read) that seems to prevent them from learning to read. This deficit might be related to the phonological loop system's development, although not enough is yet known to draw any firm conclusions (Baddeley, 1990).

One weakness of the model is that we know *least* about the component that is *most* important, namely the central executive (Hampson & Morris, 1996). It can apparently carry out an enormous variety of processing activities in different conditions. This makes it difficult to describe its *precise* function, and the idea of a single central executive might be as inappropriate as that of a unitary STM (Eysenck, 1986).

Reconceptualising long-term memory

Box 1.5 (page 18) noted that whilst Clive Wearing was severely impaired as a result of his brain damage, he was still able to use many skills and capable of learning some new ones (even though he did not know he had learnt them). These findings suggest that certain parts of his LTM were still intact, whilst others were not. This is difficult for the multi-store model to explain, since it regards LTM as a *unitary* entity.

Squire (1987) proposes a distinction between two basic types of LTM, *declarative memory* and *procedural memory*. Declarative memory has been called 'fact' memory, since it stores knowledge of specific information, for example, *knowing that* we first learned to ride a bicycle when we were three and that bicycles have two wheels. Procedural memory, by contrast, has been called 'skill' memory, since it stores our knowledge of *how to,* for example, ride a bicycle.

Declarative memory

Declarative memory can be divided into *episodic memory* (EM) and *semantic memory* (SM: Tulving, 1972, 1985).

Episodic memory

EM is an autobiographical memory system responsible for storing a record of the events, people, objects and so on which we have personally encountered. This typically includes details about times and places in which things were experienced (so knowing that we learned to ride a bicycle at the age of three is an example of EM). Although EMs have a subjective or 'self-focused' reality, most of them (such as knowing what we had for breakfast) can, at least in theory, be verified by others.

Semantic memory

SM is our store of general factual knowledge about the world, including concepts, rules and language. Tulving (1972) describes it as:

'a mental thesaurus, organised knowledge a person possesses about words and other verbal symbols, their meanings and referents'.

SM can be used without reference to where and when the knowledge was originally acquired. Most people, for example, do not remember 'learning to speak'. Rather we 'just know' our native language. SM can, however, also store information about ourselves, such as the number of sisters and brothers we have, and with memories like this we do not have to remember specific past experiences to retrieve this information. Similarly, much of our SM is built up through past experiences. For example, a 'general knowledge' about word processors is built up from past experiences with particular word processors through abstraction and generalisation (and such experiences are, of course, examples of EMs).

Originally, Tulving conceived of EM and SM as being distinct systems within LTM. However, a 'general knowledge' of word processors built up from past experiences with particular word processors suggests that a better way to view SM is as a collection of EMs (Baddeley, 1995). Also, Tulving saw EM as synonymous with *autobiographical memory* (AM), that is, our *involvement* in an event that is stored in memory. He also suggested that when we try to recall a word list as part of an experiment, EM is being assessed (since our exposure to the words was an episode in our life). However, this is not what most people understand by the term 'autobiographical' memory (Cohen, 1993). In Cohen's view, AM is a special kind of EM concerned with specific life events that have personal significance (*autobiographical EM*) as distinct from *experimental EM* which is assessed when we take part in experiments that require us to learn word lists.

Flashbulb memories

Brown & Kulik (1977) coined the termed *flashbulb memory* to refer to a special kind of EM in which we can supply a vivid and detailed recollection of where we were and what we were doing when we heard about or saw some major public event.

Box 2.4   *Flashbulb memories*

Brown & Kulik (1977) asked participants about their memories of various actual or attempted assassinations which had occurred in the previous 15 years, including those of John F. Kennedy, Martin Luther King and Robert Kennedy. They were also asked if they had flashbulb memories for more personal shocking events.

Of 80 participants, 73 reported a flashbulb memory associated with a personal shock, commonly the sudden death of a relative. John F. Kennedy's assassination was recalled most vividly, although other successful or unsuccessful assassinations also produced detailed memories. Brown and Kulik also found that flashbulb memories were more likely if an event was unexpected and personally consequential. This was shown in memories of the death of Martin Luther King. Whilst 75 per cent of black participants reported a flashbulb memory for his assassination, only 33 per cent of white participants did so. Similar findings have been obtained by Palmer *et al.* (1991) concerning memories for earthquakes amongst those living in or well away from the affected area.

The flashbulb memory phenomenon is so called because it is as though the brain has recorded an event like the scene caught in the glare of a camera's flashlight. Indeed, Brown & Kulik (1982) have argued for the existence of a special neural mechanism triggered by events that are emotionally arousing, unexpected or extremely important, resulting in the whole scene becoming 'printed' on the memory.

According to an evolutionary explanation, in prehistoric times an unexpected and consequential event threatening survival would need to be retained in memory to decrease the chance of harm from recurrence of that event. Thus, a special memory for storing events of physical significance would benefit an organism that possessed it, and this system was expanded to incorporate survival-threatening events that the organism only witnessed (Brown & Kulik, 1982).

Box 2.5   *Some important findings relating to flashbulb memories*

The durability of flashbulb memories stems from their frequent rehearsal and reconsideration after the event, and the detail of people's memories and their vividness are not necessarily signs of their accuracy (Neisser, 1982). For example, Neisser & Harsch (1992) asked college students to report how they learned about the explosion of the space shuttle *Challenger* the day after it occurred. When the students were asked about the explosion three years later, none produced an entirely accurate report, and over one-third produced a *completely* inaccurate report even though they believed it to be completely accurate.

Similar findings have been obtained in a study of recall of the 1989 Hillsborough football disaster when 95 spectators were crushed to death at a soccer match. Wright (1993) found that five months later participants could remember little and, with the passage of time, they were more likely to say they were watching television when the event occurred. According to Wright, people reconstruct events *post hoc* with recall altering over time, and such memories may not require a 'special' flashbulb mechanism.

Conway *et al.* (1994) have argued that in studies failing to find evidence of flashbulb memories, it is not entirely clear whether the events had personal consequences for the participants (a key characteristic of flashbulb memories). Since, for most British people, the resignation in 1990 of the then prime minister Margaret Thatcher was of some personal consequence, a flashbulb memory for this event might be expected. This was the case, with 86 per cent of British participants having a flashbulb memory after 11 months. Significantly, only 29 per cent of participants from other countries had a flashbulb memory after the same period of time.

Procedural memory

As noted on page 34, PM stores our knowledge of *how to*, for example, ride a bicycle. Unlike EM and AM, PM cannot be inspected consciously and its contents described to another person. When we initially learn something, it is learned and encoded declaratively, but with practice it becomes compiled into a procedural form of knowledge (Anderson, 1983). This corresponds to the distinction between controlled/automatic processing and focused/divided attention (see Gross & McIlveen, 1998). In Clive Wearing's case (see page 18), most aspects of his PM were intact, but his EM and SM were impaired. Another amnesic patient similarly affected was H.M.

Box 2.6 *The case of H.M.*

H.M. had suffered epileptic fits since the age of 16. Because they became so devastating, he underwent surgery at the age of 27 to try to cure them. The surgery, which involved removal of the hippocampus on both sides of the brain, was successful in treating the epilepsy, but left H.M. with severe amnesia. Although he had a near-normal memory for things he had learned prior to the operation, his ability to store memories of events after the surgery was very poor. Although H.M.'s STM was generally normal, he either could not transfer information into LTM or, if he could, he could not retrieve it. Thus, he had almost no knowledge of current affairs because he forgot the news shortly after having read it in a newspaper. Unless he looked at his clock, he had no idea what time of day it was.

Whilst H.M. could recognise his friends, state their names and relate stories about them, he could do so only if he knew them before his operation. Those he met afterwards remained, in effect, total strangers, and H.M. had to 'get to know them' afresh each time they came to his house. Although H.M. could learn and remember perceptual and motor skills, he had to be reminded each day just what skills he possessed. As Blakemore (1988) has remarked:

'new events, faces, phone numbers, places, now settle in his mind for just a few seconds or minutes before they slip, like water through a sieve, and are lost from his consciousness'.

When Gabrieli *et al.* (1988) gave H.M. extensive training every day for ten days in the meaning of unfamiliar words which had come into popular use since his operation, he made little progress. This failure to update SM is characteristic of amnesics (Eysenck & Keane, 1995). When new learning does occur, amnesics typically *deny* having encountered the task before, despite (as with Clive Wearing) simultaneously displaying it. Hence, the amnesic is able to demonstrate learning without the need for conscious awareness of the learning process.

Declarative memory involves conscious recollection of the past, and its adequate functioning seems to be disrupted by damage to a number of cortical and sub-cortical areas (including the temporal lobes, hippocampus, thalamus and mamillary bodies: Baddeley, 1995). N.A., a young man who suffered damage to the left side of his thalami as a result of a fencing accident, has been unable to read a book or follow a television programme, which require declarative knowledge, but has learned to ride a horse, swing a golf club and swim, which require procedural knowledge (Kaushall *et al.*, 1981). This suggests that 'fact' and 'skill' knowledge must be stored in different parts of the brain. PET studies have lent considerable support to the view that different clusters of cerebral areas are associated with primary components of memory function (Periani *et al.*, 1993: see Chapter 1).

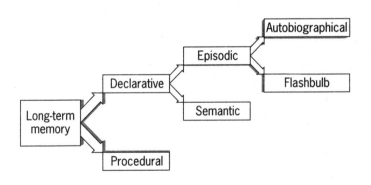

Figure 2.3 *A summary of the different kinds of LTM*

Conclusions

This chapter has considered some major alternatives to the multi-store model of memory. Whilst the levels-of-processing model sees memory as a by-product of control processes (reversing the multi-store model's view), the working memory model challenges the view of STM as unitary. Similarly, the distinction between declarative and procedural LTM accounts for cases of amnesic patients much better than the multi-store model's unitary LTM.

Summary

- Using the distinction between **maintenance** and **elaborative rehearsal**, Craik has argued that **amount** of rehearsal is less important than **type** of rehearsal.
- The multi-store model stresses the sequence of stages that information goes through as it passes from one **structural component** to another, driven by rehearsal and other **control processes**. Craik and Lockhart's **levels-of-processing model** sees memory as a by-product of these processes, specifically of perceptual analysis.
- A finite-capacity **central processor** can analyse data at either a **structural/shallow level**, a **phonemic/phonetic level** or a **semantic/deep level**. The more deeply information is processed, the better it is retained.
- **Elaboration** (the **amount** of processing) is an important determinant of retention, but the **nature** of the elaboration is more important. **Distinctive** material may be more easily remembered.
- Level of processing, elaboration and distinctiveness often co-occur, making it difficult to choose between them. However, distinctiveness is probably more important than elaboration, which is only a measure of 'how much'.
- The levels-of-processing model sees perception, attention and memory as interdependent, and challenges the assumption that any stimulus is typically processed similarly by all participants on all occasions. It is now generally accepted that **processing strategies** may help in understanding memory.
- However, the model fails to explain **why** deeper processing is more effective and **how** depth should be defined or measured

independently of actual retention scores. The **relevance** of the processing is influential, and the superior retention produced by semantic tasks could reflect the bias of retention tests towards the type of information being processed (words in both cases).

- Baddeley and Hitch criticised the multi-store model's view of STM as **unitary**. Their **working memory model** sees STM as an active store, holding information which is being manipulated. It is the 'focus of consciousness'. Working memory (WM) consists of a **central executive**, with overall control of the activities of several **slave systems**, namely the articulatory/phonological loop (inner voice), visuo-spatial scratch pad/sketch pad (inner eye) and primary acoustic store (inner ear). The limited-capacity central executive is very flexible and **modality free**, resembling a **pure attentional system**.

- It is widely accepted that attentional processes and STM are part of the **same** system, and seeing any one component as involved in apparently different tasks is a valuable insight. An important practical application of the model is in helping to explain why children have specific problems in learning to read.

- The multi-store model's view of a **unitary** LTM has difficulty explaining cases like that of Clive Wearing, whose LTM appeared to be intact in some respects but not others.

- Squire distinguishes between **declarative** ('fact') **memory**, concerned with **knowing that**, and **procedural** ('skill') **memory**, concerned with **knowing how**. Tulving distinguishes two kinds of declarative memory: **episodic memory** (EM) and **semantic memory** (SM). Rather than these being distinct systems within LTM, SM is better viewed as a collection of EMs, as when we build up general knowledge through particular past experiences.

- Tulving believed that EM is synonymous with **autobiographical memory** (AM), denoting our **involvement** in the event that is stored. However, Cohen sees AM as a special kind of EM, concerned with personally significant life events distinct from **experimental EM**.

- **Flashbulb memory** is another kind of EM, involving vivid and detailed recollection of the circumstances in which we learned of some major public event. Such memories are more likely if the event is unexpected and personally consequential.

- Brown and Kulik argue for a special neural mechanism triggered by emotionally arousing, unexpected or especially important events. This makes sense from an evolutionary perspective.

- Unlike EM and SM, **procedural memory** (PM) cannot be inspected consciously. Anderson believes that learning is initially declarative (controlled processing/focused attention), but with practice becomes compiled into a procedural form of knowledge (automatic processing/divided attention).

- Both Clive Wearing and H.M. showed a largely intact PM, whilst EM and SM were impaired. Their inability to update SM is typical of amnesics. When amnesics do learn psychomotor skills, they typically **deny** having encountered them before.

- Declarative memory involves conscious recollection of the past and is disrupted by damage to several cortical and subcortical areas. PET studies show that different clusters of cerebral areas are associated with primary components of memory function.

THE ORGANISATION OF INFORMATION IN MEMORY

Introduction and overview

3

Chapter 1 discussed the limited capacity of STM and noted that 'chunking' can apparently increase its capacity by imposing meaning on the information presented. 'Chunking' involves integrating and relating incoming information to knowledge already in LTM, *organising* it and giving it a structure it does not otherwise have. For Baddeley (1995), the secret of a good memory is, like a library, organisation, and:

'good learning typically goes with the systematic encoding of incoming material, integrating and relating it to what is already known'.

Support for the view that memory is highly organised comes from a case study reported by Hart *et al.* (1985). Two years after suffering a stroke, M.D. appeared to have made a complete recovery, the only problem being his inability to remember the names of fruits or vegetables or sort their pictures into proper categories. His ability to identify and sort types of food or vehicles into categories suggests that related information in memory is stored together, and may even be stored in specific cortical areas. This chapter looks at organisation in memory and considers models of how information is represented in semantic memory.

Some experimental studies of organisation in memory

Bousfield (1953) asked participants to learn 60 words, comprised of four categories (animals, people's names, professions and vegetables) with 15 examples of each, all mixed up. When participants free-recalled the list, they tended to cluster items from particular categories. For example, 'onion' was very likely to be recalled with other vegetables. This tendency to recall words in clusters suggested that participants had tried to organise the material (*categorical clustering*). In a more naturalistic setting, students asked to recall staff members' names tended to do so by department (Rubin & Olson, 1980).

Instructions to organise material will facilitate learning, even when participants are not trying to remember it. Mandler (1967) used a pack of 100 cards, each with a word printed on it. Participants were told to arrange the cards into categories that 'went together'. Half were told to try to remember the words, but the other half were not. Participants continued the sorting task until the cards they put into each category were 95 per cent the same from one trial to the next. When asked to remember as many words as possible, they tended to display categorical clustering. Also, those instructed just to sort the cards into categories recalled *as many* as those instructed to try and remember them, suggesting that once we become involved in working with material, we tend to organise it.

Box 3.1 *Subjective and experimenter organisation*

People will tend to create their own categories when material they are presented with does not obviously fall into categories. Tulving (1968) calls this *subjective organisation* (SO) and distinguishes it from *experimenter organisation* (EO) in which organisation is imposed by the experimenter. Bower *et al.* (1969) asked participants to learn a list of words arranged into conceptual hierarchies (Figure 3.1, see opposite). For one group, the words were organised in a hierarchical form. The other group were presented with the same words, arranged randomly. The first group recalled an average of 65 per cent of words correctly, compared with an average of only 19 per cent for the other group.

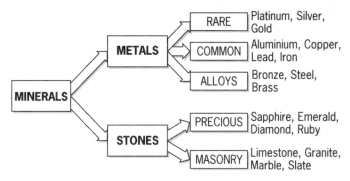

Figure 3.1 *A conceptual hierarchy as used by Bower et al. (1969)*

Imagery as a form of organisation

Imagery is the basis of many kinds of *mnemonic devices* (memory aids: see Chapter 5). Verbal material is better remembered if it can be associated in some way with a visual image. This is true for both initial learning (how the material is encoded) and retrieval. The use of imagery can be traced to the writing of Cicero, who tells the story of the Greek poet Simonides who lived around 500 BC.

Box 3.2 *The story of Simonides*

Simonides was invited to attend a banquet and give a recitation in honour of the victor of an Olympian wrestling match. Shortly after his speech, Simonides left the banqueting hall just moments before the walls, floor and ceiling collapsed, killing many guests. Such was the destruction that most of the guests were unrecognisable. Simonides, however, was able to identify them by imagining himself back in the banqueting hall and remembering that one person was sitting by a certain doorway, another by a particular column, and so on.

Simonides later applied this system to remembering other things. Whenever he wanted to remember a list of items he would visualise a building, imagine the items in various locations in sequence, and then say it. To store a speech, Simonides would group the words into concepts and leave a 'note' for each concept at a particular location in the sequence.

(From McIlveen *et al.*, 1994)

Simonides' *method of loci* ('loci' is the Greek for 'places') is still used today. One variation is the *narrative story method*. The items to be remembered are incorporated into a meaningful story which is then retold in order to remember them (Bower & Clark, 1969). A famous user of this method was a Russian journalist called Sheresheveski ('S') studied by Luria (1968). S's memory appeared to be limitless and included the ability to recall lists of more than a 100 digits and elaborate scientific formulae, even though he was not a scientist.

Box 3.3   *S's use of the narrative story method*

When S read through a long series of words, each word would elicit a graphic image, and since the series was fairly long, he had to find some way of distributing these images in a mental row or sequence. Most often (and this habit persisted throughout his life) he would 'distribute' them along some roadway or street he visualised in his mind ... Frequently he would take a mental walk along that street ... and slowly make his way down, "distributing" his images at houses, gates and in store windows ... This technique of converting a series of words into a series of graphic images explains why S could so readily reproduce a series from start to finish or in the reverse order; how he could rapidly name the word that preceded or followed one I'd selected from the walk, either from the beginning or end of the street, find the image of the object I had named and "take a look at" whatever happened to be situated on either side of it.
(From Luria, 1968)

Bower (1972) presented participants with 100 different cards one at a time, each having two unrelated words printed on it (such as 'cat' and 'brick'). Participants in one group were instructed to form mental images to *link* the unconnected words, the more vivid the image the better, whilst those in another group were simply instructed to memorise the words. Each participant was then shown a card with the first word of each pair, and asked to recall the second word. Those who used imagery recalled 80 per cent of the words, compared with only 45 per cent by the non-imagers.

Bizarre, interacting and *vivid* images are most effective (Anderson, 1995), possibly because they tend to be more distinctive or novel and take more time to form. According to Paivio's (1986) *dual-code* model of memory, memories are stored in either *sensory codes* (as visual images or sounds) or *verbal codes* (as words). Within the latter, each known word is represented by a *logogen* and within the former by *imagens*. The two systems are connected by means of *referential links* which allow a word to be associated with its relevant image (and vice versa). This can explain why it is easier to form images of *concrete* words (such as 'apple') than *abstract* words (such as 'nourishment'). Whilst abstract words may be represented in the verbal system only, concrete words may be represented in both systems (Parkin, 1993).

Eidetic imagery is a special type of mental imagery involving a persistent and clear image of some visual scene enabling it to be recalled in astonishing detail. Eidetic imagery is more common in children than adults, but only about five per cent of children display it (Haber, 1969). The ability declines with age, and has largely disappeared by early adulthood. *Eidetikers* perform no better than non-eidetic classmates on other tests of memory, and eidetic imagery appears to be an essentially perceptual phenomenon in which the coding of information is not a factor (Haber, 1980).

Semantic-network models

Semantic-network models attempt to account for the *kind* of organisation that occurs in memory. Different models share a concern with how meaningful material (rather than meaningless material, such as nonsense syllables) is organised, and they all assume that semantic organisation is best thought of in terms of multiple, interconnected associations, relationships or pathways. The models assume that information is embedded in an organised, structured network composed of semantic units and their functional relationships to one another (Houston *et al.*, 1991).

Hierarchical-network models

Collins and Quillian's model

Collins & Quillian's (1969, 1972) *teachable language comprehender* is primarily concerned with *lexical memory* (memory for particular words rather than grammar or sentences).

Box 3.4 *The hierarchical network model of semantic memory*

Collins and Quillian see SM as organised in the form of a hierarchical network. Major concepts are represented as *nodes*, each node having several properties or features associated with it. Each node is also associated with other concepts elsewhere in the hierarchy.

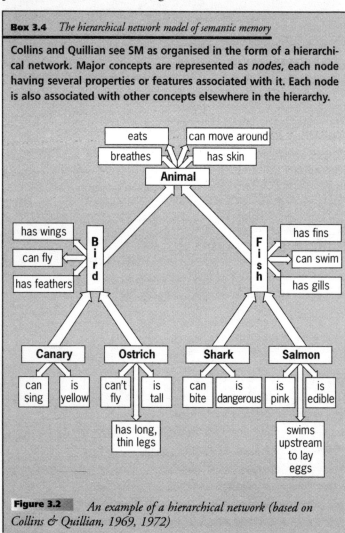

Figure 3.2 *An example of a hierarchical network (based on Collins & Quillian, 1969, 1972)*

In Figure 3.2 (see previous page), the concept 'animal' and the properties or features associated with animals appear at the top of the hierarchy. The concept 'animal' is also associated with the concepts of 'bird' and 'fish' which appear at the next level in the hierarchy. In turn, these concepts are associated with yet other concepts lower down in the hierarchy. Thus, the 'bird' concept is associated with 'canary' and ostrich' whilst the 'fish' concept is associated with 'shark' and salmon'. Since almost all birds have wings, feathers and can fly, it is not necessary for these features to appear lower down the hierarchy as properties of canaries and ostriches. This hierarchical rrangement means that large amounts of information can be stored very economically.

Experimental tests of the model typically involve *sentence verification tasks*. In these, participants are given a sentence such as 'A canary can sing' or 'A canary can fly' and asked to verify whether the sentence is true or not. The time taken to verify each sentence is recorded. The model predicts that with a sentence like 'A canary can sing', reaction time should be shorter than with the sentence 'A canary can fly'. This is because the property 'can sing' is associated with the concept 'canary', whilst 'can fly' is associated with the concept 'bird', one level further up the hierarchy. A sentence like 'A canary breathes' should take even longer to verify, since this involves crossing two levels of the hierarchy.

Consistent with their model, Collins and Quillian found that the time taken to decide whether a statement was true increased as a function of the number of levels of the hierarchy that had to be crossed to verify it.

Box 3.5 *Alternative explanations of Collins and Quillian's data*

- It might take longer to verify 'A canary is an animal' because there are more animals than birds. In other words, their findings could be explained in terms of the *category size* and reaction time relationship.
- The sentence 'A canary is a bird' (in which the canary is a *typical* instance) is verified more quickly than 'An ostrich is a bird' (an

atypical instance). Since both sentences involve crossing the same number of levels, Collins and Quillian's model would predict no difference in verification time for the two sentences (Baddeley, 1990).

● Conrad (1972) found that response time may reflect the *relative frequency* with which certain attributes are commonly associated with a particular concept. When frequency was controlled for, there was no evidence for longer response times to categories supposedly stored at a higher level. This suggests that 'semantic relatedness' (the attributes commonly associated with particular concepts) could account for the original findings. Conrad's data suggest that not all attributes of a concept are *equally important* or salient.

● Rips *et al.* (1973) found that it takes longer to verify 'A bear is a mammal' than 'A bear is an animal'. Since 'animal' is higher up in the hierarchy than 'mammal', this is the opposite of what Collins and Quillian's model predicts.

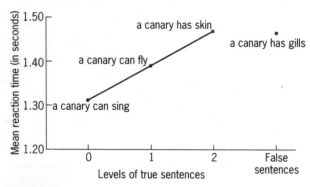

Figure 3.3   *Data from Collins and Quillian's sentence verification tasks*

According to Bower & Hilgard (1981):

'a realistic memory, of course, contains thousands of ... concepts, each with very many connections, so that the actual topographical representation would look like a huge "wiring diagram"'.

In Lindsay & Norman's (1977) model, just a fragment of information enables many questions to be answered. For example, if the system was asked to compare the similarities and differences between beer and wine, it could do this (see Gross & McIlveen, 1997).

Matrix models

Broadbent *et al.* (1978) gave participants a list of 16 words to remember. For the control group, the words were presented randomly, whilst for one experimental group, they were organised hierarchically. A second experimental group was presented with the words in the form of a matrix.

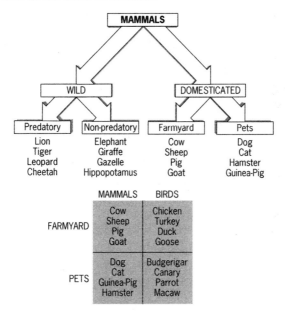

Figure 3.4 *The hierarchical organisation of words in Broadbent et al.'s experiment (a), and the same words presented in matrix form (b)*

The two experimental groups' participants remembered significantly more words than those in the control group. However, the experimental groups did not differ from one another, suggesting that both hierarchical and matrix organisations are equally helpful in remembering.

Feature models

Smith *et al.*'s (1974) *feature approach* is concerned with our ability to decide whether certain nouns belong to certain categories (see Rips *et al.*'s 1973 study in Box 3.5). For example, suppose we are asked to verify 'A cat is an animal'. For Smith *et al.*, the crucial factor is not the spatial relationship between the two concepts, but the number of *features* they have in common. A cat and an animal have a large number of shared features and as a result, it should not take long to verify the sentence. Also, it should not take long to verify 'A cat is sand', since these two concepts have *nothing* in common.

Sometimes, though, the number of common attributes is *intermediate*. In 'A mould is a plant', the two concepts share some features, but it is difficult to generate enough to enable a quick decision to be reached. In such circumstances we look at *defining features* (a necessary and sufficient condition for reaching a decision) and *characteristic features* (a typical attribute of an item belonging to a category, but not itself sufficient to determine whether something belongs to a category). For example, any animal that has feathers is a bird, since there are no featherless birds and no non-birds that have feathers. However, whilst birds characteristically fly, not all do, and some things that do fly are not birds. When the number of common attributes belonging to a category is intermediate, and a decision is difficult to reach, we consider *only* defining features, which inevitably slows down the decision process (Hampton, 1979). This feature approach to SM can, therefore, explain some of the data that are difficult for Collins and Quillian's model.

Spreading-activation models

Collins & Loftus (1975) proposed a revised network model, intended to address the criticisms made of Collins and Quillian's hierarchical model.

Box 3.6 *Differences between the spreading activation model and Collins and Quillian's hierarchical network model*

- The network is not limited to hierarchical relationships between concepts.
- The *semantic distance* between concepts varies. The greater the distance, the weaker the relationship between the concepts. Thus, highly related concepts are located close together.
- When a particular item is processed, activation spreads out along the pathways from a concept in all directions. An activated item can be more easily processed (retrieved, judged, recognised or evaluated) than an unactivated one.

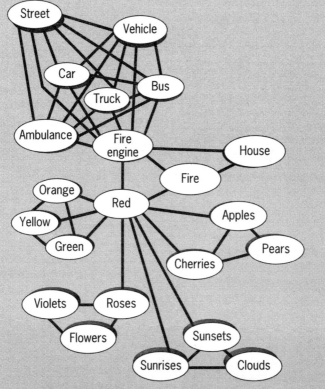

Figure 3.5 *An example of a spreading-activation model. The length of each line (or link) represents the degree of association between particular concepts (based on Collins & Loftus, 1975)*

Several studies have provided data consistent with the model (e.g. Jones & Anderson, 1987). In *lexical-decision experiments*, participants are first shown a *prime*, such as the word 'dog'. Then, a *target* word is shown for a very brief period of time. This may be related to the prime word (e.g. 'dalmatian'), unrelated (e.g. 'banana') or even a nonsense word (e.g. 'grilf'). Participants have to judge whether the target word actually is a word or whether it belongs to a certain category. The speed with which a decision is reached is increased the closer the relationship between the target and prime. In terms of the spreading-activation model, this is because the prime activates material in the semantic network, and the closer the prime is to the target, the more activated and more easily processed it is.

However, Johnson-Laird *et al.* (1984) observe that there are many examples where the interpretation offered by the network will tend, in actual discourse, to be overridden by the constraints of real-world knowledge. Consider, for example, the sentence 'The ham sandwich was eaten by the soup'. Whilst this may seem nonsensical, for waiters and waitresses (who often label customers according to their orders) the sentence is quite understandable. This 'failure to escape from the maze of symbols into the world' is called the *symbolic fallacy*: a person has to know the relationship between symbols and what they refer to.

Schemas

Clearly, SM must contain structures much larger than the simple concepts considered by the models so far discussed. This 'larger unit' is the *schema*, a term introduced to memory research by Bartlett (see Chapter 1, page 4). Bartlett was the first to recognise that memory is a *reconstructive* process in which information already stored affects the remembering of other events. He found that people frequently add or delete details to make new information more consistent with their conception of the world. So, for Bartlett, memory is not like a computer, with output matching input, but an 'imaginative reconstruction' of experience.

Schemas provide us with preconceived expectations, operating in a 'top-down' way to help interpret the 'bottom-up' flow of information reaching the senses. Schemas help to make the world more predictable. They can, however, also lead to significant distortions in memory processes, because they have a powerful effect on the way in which memories for events are encoded (Crooks & Stein, 1991). For example, Allport & Postman (1947) showed white participants a picture of two men evidently engaged in an argument.

Figure 3.6   *The stimulus material used by Allport & Postman (1947). The two men are engaged in an argument. The better-dressed man is black, and the white man has a cut throat razor in his left hand*

After briefly looking at the picture, participants were asked to describe the scene to someone who had not seen it. This person was then required to pass the information on to another person, and so on. As the information was passed, so features of it changed, the most important being that the knife was reported as being in the black man's hand.

Neisser (1981) studied the testimony given by John Dean, a key figure in the Watergate conspiracy. Dean testified to a committee (that was trying to determine whether President Nixon had been involved in a plan to 'bug' the Democratic National Committee headquarters) about an event that had occurred nine months earlier.

Box 3.7 *Neisser's (1981) analysis of John Dean's testimony*

According to Dean:

'When I arrived at the Oval Office, I found Haldeman and the President. The President asked me to sit down. Both men appeared to be in very good spirits, and my reception was warm and cordial. The President then told me that Bob [Haldeman] had kept him posted on my handling of the Watergate case. The President told me that I had done a good job and he appreciated how difficult a task it had been and the President was pleased that the case had stopped with Liddy'.

A comparison of this statement with transcripts of the tape-recording Nixon *secretly* made of the meeting revealed the following discrepancies:

- Nixon did not ask Dean to sit down.
- Nixon did not say that Haldeman had 'kept him posted'.
- No compliment was paid by Nixon on the job Dean had done.
- Nixon did not say that he 'appreciated how difficult a task it had been'.
- There was no reference made to Liddy and the case by Nixon.

Neisser suggests that Dean's specific recollection might have come from the schema that describes what generally happens when people enter a room (viz., the host greets the guest, and the guest is invited to sit down).

Schemas can also powerfully enhance memory, as shown by Bransford & Johnson (1972), whose participants were asked to read the passage overleaf.

Box 3.8 *The passage read by participants in Bransford & Johnson's (1972) experiment*

The procedure is actually quite simple. First you arrange items into several different groups. Of course, one pile might be sufficient, depending on how much there is to do. If you have to go some-where else due to lack of facilities, that is the next step; otherwise you are pretty well set. It is important not to overdo things. That is, it is better to do a few things at once than too many. In the short run, this may not seem important but complications can easily arise. A mistake can be expensive as well. At first, the whole procedure will seem complicated. Soon, however, it will become just another fact of life. It is difficult to see any end to the necessity of this task in the immediate future, but then one can never tell. After the pro-cedure is completed, one arranges the material into different groups again. They then can be put into their appropriate places. Eventually, they will be used once more and the whole cycle will have to be repeated. However, that is part of life.

Participants found the passage difficult to understand and later recalled only a few of its 18 distinct ideas. This was because they could not relate the material to what they already knew (they lacked an appropriate schema). However, when another group of participants were told in advance that the passage was about *washing clothes*, they found it more understandable and recalled twice as many ideas as the first group.

Schema theories

Schema theory is one of the most influential approaches to understanding the complex pattern of remembering and forget-ting (Cohen, 1993). Several schema theories have been advanced (e.g. Rumelhart, 1975; Schank, 1975; Schank & Abelson, 1977), and there is considerable overlap between them.

Box 3.9 *Similarities between schema theories*

● Schemas are viewed as 'packets of information' consisting of a fixed compulsory value and a variable (or optional) value. Our

> schema for buying things has fixed slots for the exchange of money and goods, and variable slots for the amount of money and nature of the goods. In some cases, a slot may be left unspecified and can often be filled with a 'default value, or 'best guess' given the available information.
>
> ● Schemas are not mutually exclusive but can combine to form systems. A schema for a picnic, for example, might be part of a larger system of schemas including 'meals' and 'outings'.
>
> ● Schemas can relate to *abstract* ideologies and concepts (such as 'justice') and *concrete* objects (such as the appearance of a face).
>
> ● Schemas represent knowledge and experience of the world rather than definitions and rules about the world.
>
> ● Schemas are active recognition devices which enable us to make sense of ambiguous and unfamiliar information in terms of our existing knowledge and understanding.

Schank and Abelson argue that we develop schemas (or *scripts*) which represent the sequence of actions when carrying out commonly experienced social events, such as going to a restaurant and the objects and people likely to be encountered. These scripts enable us to fill in much of the detail which might not be specified in a piece of information. Consider, for example, the sentences 'We had a tandoori chicken at the Taj Mahal last night. The service was slow, and we almost missed the start of the play.' This can only be interpreted by bringing in additional information (Baddeley, 1990). We need schemas to predict what would happen next and to fill in those aspects of the event which are left implicit. Such scripts are essential ways of summarising common cultural assumptions. This helps us understand text and discourse, and enables us to predict future events and behave appropriately in given social situations.

Schank & Abelson (1977) built their scripts into a computer program called *SAM*. The program, whose 'restaurant script' is shown in Table 3.1, can evidently 'answer' questions and 'understand' stories about restaurants.

Table 3.1 *A simplified version of Schank and Abelson's schematic representation of activities involved in going to a restaurant*

Name	Restaurant
Props	Tables, menu, food, bill, money, tip
Entry conditions	Customer is hungry
	Customer has money
Roles	Customer, waiter, cook, cashier, owner
Results	Customer has less money
	Owner has more money
	Customer is not hungry
Scene 1	**Entering**
	Customer enters restaurant
	Customer looks for table
	Customer decides where to sit
	Customer goes to table
	Customer sits down
Scene 2	**Ordering**
	Customer picks up menu
	Customer looks at menu
	Customer decides on food
	Customer signals waiter
	Waiter comes to table
	Customer orders food
	Waiter goes to cook
	Waiter gives food order to cook
	Cook prepares food
Scene 3	**Eating**
	Waiter gives food to customer
	Customer eats food
Scene 4	**Exiting**
	Waiter prepares bill
	Waiter goes over to customer
	Waiter gives bill to customer
	Customer gives tip to waiter
	Customer goes to cashier
	Customer gives money to cashier
	Customer leaves restaurant

(Based on Bower *et al.*, 1979)

There are certain actions and events that form part of people's knowledge about what is involved in going into a restaurant, and these broadly agree with Schank and Abelson's restaurant script (Bower *et al.*, 1979). Also, when people are asked to recall a passage of text concerning 'restaurant behaviour', they falsely recall aspects which were not explicitly included but which are consistent with a 'restaurant script', *and* change the order of events so as to make them consistent with such a script (exactly as Bartlett would have predicted).

An evaluation of schema theories

According to Cohen (1993), the whole idea of a schema appears to be so vague as to be of little practical use. Also, schema theories tend to emphasise the inaccuracies of memory and overlook the fact that complex events are sometimes remembered very accurately (especially their unexpected and unusual aspects). Finally, theories have little to say about the acquisition of schemas. Without schemas, we are unable to interpret new experiences, and we need new experiences in order to build up schemas (Cohen, 1993).

Schank's (1982) *dynamic-memory theory* attempts to take account of the dynamic aspects of memory and is a more elaborate and flexible version of his original theory. It tries to clarify the relationship between general knowledge schemas and memories for specific episodes, based on a hierarchical arrangement of memory representations. At the bottom of the hierarchy are *memory organisation packets* (MOPs) which store specific details about specific events. At higher levels, the representations become more and more general and schema-like. MOPs are not usually stored for very long, and become 'absorbed' into the 'event schemas' that store those features common to repeated experiences. Details of unusual or atypical events, however, are retained (Cohen, 1993).

According to Alba & Hasher (1983) and Bahrick (1984), whilst there is some evidence for schema theories, schemas themselves are unlikely to be involved in the retrieval of general knowledge, such as remembering one's name, facts and rules. Bahrick's own research concerns memory which closely resembles the original content (*replicative memory*: Bahrick, 1984). Even people who studied a particular language (Spanish) 50 years earlier, and have never used it since, remembered 'large portions of the originally acquired information'. This suggests that at least some types of information can be stored for very long periods of time and recalled in their *original* form.

Conclusions

Evidence supports the view that memory is highly organised. The organisation of information can be achieved by a variety of methods, and several models have been proposed to explain the kind of organisation that occurs in memory, although no one model is completely supported by research.

Summary

- Chunking is a way of **organising** information by giving it a structure it does not otherwise have. Organisation is the secret of a good memory.
- Bousfield found that participants free-recalled randomly presented words in clusters (**categorical clustering**), despite not being told of the categories into which they fell. This suggested that they had tried to organise the words.
- Mandler showed that instructions to organise material will facilitate learning, even when participants are not trying to remember it. Not only did categorical clustering occur, but participants instructed just to sort the cards into categories remembered as many as those instructed to remember them.
- Tulving distinguishes between **subjective organisation** (SO), and **experimenter organisation** (EO). Bower *et al.* showed that when words were presented in the form of conceptual **hierarchies**, they were recalled significantly better than when they were presented randomly.
- **Imagery** represents a form of organisation and is the basis of many kinds of **mnemonic devices**. The use of imagery can be

traced to the ancient Greek poet Simonides, who used the **method of loci**, a modern form of which is the **narrative story method**.

- Bower found that participants instructed to **link** pairs of unrelated words through visual images performed much better on a recall test than those simply instructed to memorise the words. **Bizarre, interacting** and **vivid** images are most effective, possibly because they are more distinctive.

- According to Paivio, imagery's effectiveness can be explained in terms of a **dual-code model of memory** (with memories being stored as **imagens** or **logogens**). The two systems are connected by **referential links**, which explains why it is easier to form images of **concrete** than **abstract** words.

- **Semantic-network models** attempt to identify the kind of organisation that occurs in memory. They assume that information is embedded in an organised structural network composed of semantic units and their functional relationships to one another.

- Collins and Quillian's **teachable language comprehender** is mainly concerned with the **nature of lexical memory**. SM is organised as a **hierarchical** network, with major concepts represented as **nodes**, each having several properties or features associated with it and linked with concepts at a lower level in the hierarchy. These, in turn, are linked with concepts lower down in the hierarchy.

- Using **sentence verification tasks**, Collins and Quillian confirmed the model's prediction that the more levels that have to be crossed, the longer it takes to verify a sentence's truth or falsity. However, this could be explained in terms of the relationship between **category size** and reaction time, and some members of a category are much more **typical** than others. Response time may also reflect 'semantic relatedness'. Different attributes of a particular concept may not be equally important.

- Broadbent *et al.* found that participants presented with words in either a hierarchical or matrix form remembered significantly more of them than participants presented with the words in a random order. However, the first two groups did equally well, suggesting that SM may be organised in the form of **matrices**.

- According to Smith *et al.*'s **feature model**, the crucial factor in deciding whether a sentence is true is the number of features the concepts have in common. When the number of common features is **intermediate**, the task becomes more difficult.

- The network in Collins and Loftus's **spreading-activation model** is not limited to hierarchical relationships between concepts. The **semantic distance** between concepts varies, and when a particular item is processed, activation spreads out along the pathways from a concept in all directions.

- SM must contain structures considerably larger than the simple concepts proposed by the various semantic network models. **Schemas** represent this larger unit, providing preconceived expectations and making the world more predictable. However, they may also distort our memories.

- **Schema theories** share a common view of schemas as interrelated 'packets of information ' comprising both a fixed compulsory value and a variable or optional value. They can refer to both abstract concepts and concrete objects and are active recognition devices which help make sense of ambiguous or unfamiliar information.

- Schank and Abelson believe that we develop scripts regarding the sequence of actions involved in commonly experienced social events. Scripts help us to fill in missing details by allowing us to predict what would happen next, as well as enabling us to behave appropriately in given social situations.

- Schema theories tend to emphasise the limitations of memory and overlook the sometimes accurate recall of complex events. Schank's **dynamic-memory theory** identifies the relationship between general knowledge schemas and memories for specific episodes.

THEORIES OF FORGETTING

4

Introduction and overview

Forgetting can occur at the encoding, storage or retrieval stage. A crucial distinction in forgetting is between *availability* and *accessibility*. Availability refers to whether or not the material has been stored in the first place, whereas accessibility refers to being able to retrieve what has been stored. In terms of the multi-store model of memory, since information must be transferred from STM to LTM for permanent storage, availability mainly concerns STM and the transfer of information from it into LTM. Accessibility, by contrast, mainly concerns LTM. Forgetting may be caused by many factors, including physical trauma and drug abuse which cause actual brain damage (Clifford, 1991). This chapter reviews the various *psychological* explanations of forgetting and their related evidence.

Motivated-forgetting theory

According to Freud, forgetting is a motivated process rather than a failure of learning or other processes. *Repression* refers to an unconscious process in which certain memories are made inaccessible. Those memories likely to elicit guilt, embarrassment, shame or anxiety are repressed from consciousness as a form of *defence mechanism*.

Box 4.1 *A case of repression*

Freud (1901) reported the case of a man who continually forgot the line that followed 'with a white sheet' even though he was familiar with the poem from which it came. Freud found that the man associated 'white sheet' with the linen sheet that is placed over a corpse. An overweight friend of the man's had recently died from a heart attack, and the man was worried that because he was a little overweight, and his grandfather had died of heart disease, the

---

same fate would befall him. For Freud, the apparently innocent forgetting of a line from a poem involved the repression of unconscious conflicts over a fear of death.

There is little doubt that traumatic experiences can produce memory disturbances, but there is greater doubt as to whether a Freudian explanation best accounts for them (Anderson, 1995). Clinical evidence exists which is consistent with Freud's theory, an example being *psychogenic amnesia* (amnesia which does not have a physiological cause). One common form of this is loss of memory for events occurring over some particular time frame (*event-specific amnesia*). Psychogenic amnesia is linked to stressful events, and may last for hours or years, although it may disappear as suddenly as it appeared, which is difficult for motivated-forgetting theory to explain.

According to Parkin (1993), repressive mechanisms may play a beneficial role in enabling people experiencing *post-traumatic stress disorder* to adjust. For example, Kaminer & Lavie (1991) found that Holocaust survivors judged to be better adjusted to their experiences were less able to recall their dreams when woken from REM sleep than those judged to be less well adjusted. However, when the term 'repression' is used, it does not necessarily imply a strict Freudian interpretation. Instead, Parkin sees the use of the word as:

'simply acknowledging that memory has the ability to render part of its contents inaccessible as a means of coping with distressing experiences [and that] the mechanism by which memory achieves this ... is an elusive one'.

Box 4.2 *Recovered memories and false memory syndrome*

One difficulty with accepting recovered *memories* as literal interpretations of past events (such as child sexual abuse) is that they might (supposedly) have happened at a very early age, when experience is not verbalised as it is later on in life (British Psychological

Society/BPS, 1995). Child sexual abuse which occurs before the age of four and doesn't continue beyond that age might not be retrievable in a narrative form (describable in words). Very early memories are implicit rather than explicit and are reflected in behaviour outside conscious awareness. This means that we don't need repression to explain the 'forgetting' of childhood experiences, but it also implies that some recovered memories could be either false or inaccurate.

The BPS's survey of 810 chartered psychologists indicated that 90 per cent believed recovered memories to be sometimes or 'essentially' correct, a very small percentage believed that they are always correct, about 66 per cent believed that they are possible, and 14 per cent believed that one of their own clients has experienced false memories.

According to Loftus (1997), false memories can be constructed by combining actual memories with the content of suggestions from others. This may result in *source confusion*, in which the content and the source become dissociated. However:

'... although experimental work on the creation of false memories may raise doubt about the validity of long-buried memories, such as repeated trauma, it in no way disproves them ... '(Loftus, 1997).

Distortion and decay theories

The Gestalt theory

The Gestalt theory of forgetting (also known as *systematic distortion of the memory trace*) is closely related to the Gestalt theory of perception (see Gross & McIlveen, 1998). Gestalt theorists claim that memories undergo *qualitative changes* over time rather than being lost completely, and become distorted towards a 'better', more regular, symmetrical form. Several studies have claimed to support this theory, mainly using participants' reproduction by drawings of material seen earlier (e.g. Wulf, 1922; Irwin & Seidenfeld, 1937; James, 1958). Such studies claim that genuine changes in memory occur with the passage of time.

However, several researchers (e.g. Baddeley, 1968) have found that such results can be explained in terms of experimental artefacts and biases (such as a limitation in participants' abilities to accurately draw the figures they had seen). The Gestalt theory of forgetting, then, has proved to be 'both experimentally and theoretically sterile' (Baddeley, 1976).

Decay theory

Decay (or *trace decay*) theory attempts to explain why forgetting increases with time. Clearly, memories must be stored somewhere, the most obvious location being the brain. Presumably, some sort of structural change (the *engram*) occurs when learning takes place. According to decay theory, metabolic processes occur over time which degrade the engram (unless it is maintained by repetition and rehearsal), resulting in the memory contained within it becoming unavailable.

Hebb (1949) argued that whilst learning is taking place, the engram which will eventually be formed is very delicate and liable to disruption (the *active trace*). With learning, it grows stronger until a permanent engram is formed (the *structural trace*) through neurochemical and neuroanatomical changes. The active trace corresponds roughly to STM, and according to decay theory forgetting from STM is due to the disruption of the active trace. Although Hebb did not apply the idea of decay to LTM, other researchers have argued that it can explain such forgetting if it is assumed that decay occurs through *disuse*. So, if certain knowledge or skills are not used or practised for long time periods, the engram corresponding to them will eventually decay away (Loftus & Loftus, 1980).

However, even if they are not practised, certain motor skills (such as driving a car or playing the piano) are not lost (as shown by Bahrick, 1984: see page 61). Also, even if people haven't used something like algebra for years, it can be remembered *if* they follow a 'refresher' course at college (Bahrick & Hall, 1991). The ability of a delirious person to remember a foreign language not spoken since childhood also testifies against a simple 'decay through disuse' explanation of forgetting.

Peterson & Peterson's (1959) study (see Chapter 1, page 12) is often taken as evidence for the role of decay in STM forgetting. If such decay did occur, then we would expect poorer recall of information with the passage of time, which is exactly what the Petersons reported. However, the difficulty with the Petersons' study in particular, and decay theory in general, is that other possible effects need to be excluded before an account based on decay can be accepted.

The ideal way to study decay's role in forgetting would be to have people receive information and then do *nothing* physical or mental for a period of time. If recall was poorer with the passage of time, it would be reasonable to suggest that decay had occurred. Such an experiment is, of course, impossible. However, Jenkins & Dallenbach (1924) were the first to attempt to *approximate* it.

Box 4.3 *Jenkins & Dallenbach's (1924) experiment*

Participants learnt a list of ten nonsense syllables. In one condition, they then went to sleep immediately, approximating to the ideal 'do nothing' state. Others continued with their normal activities. After intervals of one, two, four or eight hours, participants were tested for their recall of the syllables.

The period spent asleep did not result in greater forgetting (see Figure 4.1, page 70), which led Jenkins and Dallenbach to conclude that:

'forgetting is not so much a matter of decay of old impressions and associations as it is a matter of interference, inhibition or obliteration of the old by the new'.

Although some data indicate that neurological breakdown occurs with age and disease (such as Alzheimer's disease), it is generally accepted that neurological decay is *not* the major cause of forgetting from LTM (Solso, 1995).

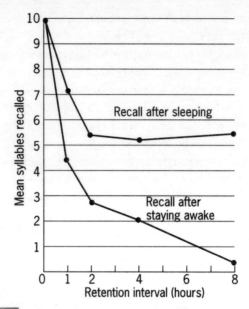

Figure 4.1 *Mean number of syllables recalled by participants in Jenkins and Dallenbach's experiment*

Interference theory

According to interference theory, forgetting is influenced more by what we do before or after learning than by the passage of time. In *retroactive interference* (or *retroactive inhibition*), later learning interferes with the recall of earlier learning. Suppose a person originally learned to drive in a manual car, then learned to drive an automatic car. When returning to a manual car, the person might try to drive it as though it was an automatic.

In *proactive interference* (or *proactive inhibition*), earlier learning interferes with the recall of later learning. Suppose a person learned to drive a car in which the indicator lights are turned on using the stalk on the left of the steering wheel, and the windscreen wipers by the stalk on the right. After passing the driving test, the person then buys a car in which this arrangement is reversed. Proactive interference would be shown by the windscreen wipers being activated just before the person signalled his or her intention to turn left or right!

Interference theory has been extensively studied in the laboratory using *paired-associates lists*, and the usual procedure for studying interference effects is shown in Figure 4.2.

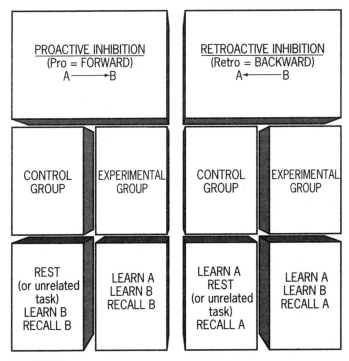

Figure 4.2 *Experimental procedures for investigating retroactive and proactive interference*

Usually, the first member of each pair in list A is the same as in list B, but the second member of each pair is different in the two lists. In retroactive interference (RI), the learning of the second list interferes with recall of the original list (working *backwards* in time). In proactive interference (PI), the learning of the original list interferes with recall of the later learned second list (working *forwards* in time).

Interference offers an alternative explanation of Peterson & Peterson's (1959) data (see page 12). Having noted that the Petersons administered two *practice trials* before their test, Keppel & Underwood (1962) looked at what happened after these trials in the actual experiment. They found that the first two trials did have an effect on those that followed, in that there was no evidence of forgetting on the first trial, some on the second and yet more on the third. Whilst other researchers (e.g. Baddeley & Scott, 1971) have shown that forgetting *can* occur on the first trial (supporting decay theory), Keppel and Underwood's finding that performance did not decline until the second trial suggests the occurrence of proactive interference in the Petersons' experiment.

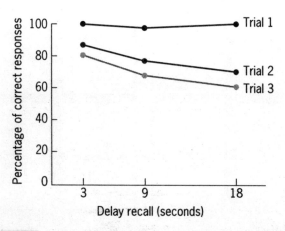

Figure 4.3   *Mean percentage of items correctly recalled on trials 1, 2 and 3 for various delay times (Based on Keppel & Underwood, 1962)*

Probably the most important cause of proactive interference is interference with *retrieval*. Like Keppel and Underwood, Wickens (1972) found that participants became increasingly poor at retaining information in STM on successive trials. However, when the *category* of information was changed, participants performed as well as on the first list. So, performance with lists of numbers was increasingly poor over trials, but if the task was changed to lists of letters, it improved. This is called *release from proactive inhibition.*

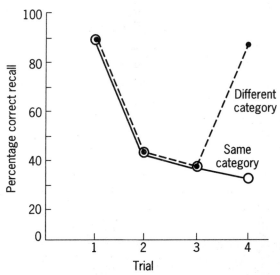

Figure 4.4   *The effect on recall of being presented with a list of stimuli from a different category*

Release from proactive inhibition occurs when people are told about a change of category *either before or after it occurs* (Gardiner *et al.*, 1972). This is important because it indicates that the major cause of proactive interference must be interference with the retrieval of information from STM rather than with its storage, since telling participants about a category change *after* they have heard the words cannot possibly affect the way those words are stored in STM. It can, however, affect the way in which participants attempt to retrieve the words.

The strongest support for interference theory comes from laboratory studies. However, learning in such studies does not occur in the same way as it does in the real world where learning of potentially interfering material is spaced out over time. In the laboratory, though, learning is artificially compressed in time, and this maximises the likelihood of interference occurring (Baddeley, 1990). Laboratory studies of interference, therefore, lack *ecological validity*.

Also, most laboratory-based investigations supportive of interference theory have used nonsense syllables as the stimulus material, and when meaningful material is used, interference is more difficult to demonstrate (Solso, 1995). When people have to learn the response 'bell' to the stimulus 'woj', the word 'bell' is not actually learned in the laboratory since it is already part of people's *semantic memory* (SM). Rather, what has to be learned is that 'bell' is the response word to 'woj', and this is stored in *episodic memory*, since the learning is taking place in a specific laboratory situation. Experimental studies of interference are largely based on episodic memory and hence interference effects apply only to that type of LTM. Since SM is much more stable and structured, it is also much more resistant to the effects of interference (Solso, 1995).

However, there is some evidence of interference outside the laboratory. For example, Gunter *et al.* (1980) found that if participants viewed successive television news broadcasts, they experienced retroactive interference, whilst Chandler (1989) showed that if students have to study more than one subject in the same time frame, subjects that are as dissimilar as possible should be chosen to minimise the possibility of interference occurring (see Chapter 5, page 98).

Displacement theory

In a *limited capacity* STM system, forgetting might occur through displacement. When the system is 'full', the oldest material in it would be displaced ('pushed out') by incoming new material. This possibility was explored by Waugh & Norman (1965) using the *serial probe task*. Participants were presented with 16 digits at the rate of either one or four per second. One of the digits (the 'probe') was then repeated and participants had to say which digit *followed* the probe.

Presumably, if the probe was one of the digits at the beginning of the list, the probability of recalling the digit that followed would be small, because later digits would have displaced earlier ones from the system. However, if the probe was presented towards the end of the list, the probability of recalling the digit that followed it would be high, since the last digits to be presented would still be available in STM.

When the number of digits following the probe was small, recall was good, but when it was large, recall was poor. This is consistent with the idea that the earlier digits are displaced by later ones. Waugh and Norman also found that recall was generally better with the faster (four-per-second) presentation rate, which is consistent with decay theory. Since less time had elapsed between presentation of the digits and the probe in the four-per-second condition, there would be less opportunity for those digits to have decayed away.

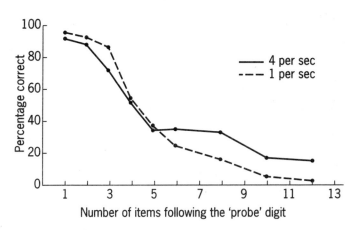

Figure 4.5 *Data from Waugh and Norman's serial probe experiment*

Waugh and Norman's findings were confirmed by Shallice (1967), although Shallice found that elapsed time was *less* important than the number of subsequent items. Despite such evidence, it is unclear that displacement is a process distinct from either decay or interference or, indeed, some combination of the two.

Retrieval-failure theory

According to retrieval-failure theory, memories cannot be recalled because the correct *retrieval cues* are not being used. The role of retrieval cues is demonstrated by the *tip-of-the-tongue phenomenon*, in which we know that we know something but cannot retrieve it at that particular point in time (Brown & McNeill, 1966).

Brown and McNeill gave participants dictionary definitions of unfamiliar words and asked them to provide the words themselves. Most participants either knew the word or knew that they did not know it. Some, however, were sure they knew the word but could not recall it (it was on the tip of their tongue). About half could give the word's first letter and the number of syllables, and often offered words which sounded like the word or had a similar meaning. This suggests that the required words were in memory, but the absence of a correct retrieval cue prevented them from being recalled.

Box 4.4   *An example of a tip-of-the-tongue test*

For each of the six examples below, try to identify the word that fits each definition. You may find that you cannot think of the word, yet you know that it is on the verge of coming to you. When a word is on the tip-of-your-tongue, see if you can prompt its retrieval by writing down (1) the number of syllables, (2) the initial letter, (3) words which sound similar, and (4) words of similar meaning.

1 A small boat used in the harbours and rivers of Japan and China, rowed with a scull from the stern, and often having a sail.
2 A navigational instrument used to measure angular distances at sea, especially the altitude of the sun, moon and stars.
3 Favouritism, especially governmental patronage extended to relatives.
4 The common cavity into which the various ducts of the body open in certain fishes, reptiles, birds and mammals.

---

5 An opaque, greyish, waxy secretion from the intestines of the sperm whale, sometimes found floating on the ocean or lying on the shore, and used in making perfumes.

6 An extending portion of a building, usually semicircular with half a dome; especially the part of a church where the altar is located.

(Based on Brown & McNeill, 1966, and adapted from Carlson, 1987. The answers are given on page 80)

Tulving & Pearlstone (1966) read participants lists of varying numbers of words (12, 24 or 48) containing categories of one, two or four exemplars per list along with the category name. Participants were instructed only to try to remember the exemplars (such as category name = animal, exemplar = dog). Half the participants free-recalled the words and wrote these down on a blank piece of paper. The other half were provided with the category names. Those participants given the category names recalled significantly more words, and the difference was most pronounced on the 48-item list. However, when the category names were provided for those who had written their responses on the blank sheet of paper, their recall improved, indicating that the category names helped to make information that was available for recall accessible.

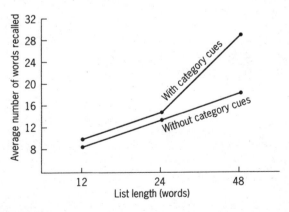

Figure 4.6 *Average number of words recalled with and without category cues in Tulving & Pearlstone's (1966) experiment.*

Tulving (1968) has also shown that retrieval failure offers a better account of forgetting from LTM than either decay or interference theory.

Box 4.5   *Tulving's (1968) experiment*

Participants were shown a list of words and then asked to write down as many as they could remember in any order they liked. Later, and without being presented with the list again or seeing the words they had written down previously, participants were asked for a second time to recall as many of the words as possible. Even later, they were asked to recall for a third time the words on the original list.

Table 4.1   *Hypothetical results*

Trial 1	Trial 2	Trial 3
Table	Table	Table
Driver	Escalator	Driver
Escalator	Apple	Escalator
Apple	Railway	Apple
Railway	Pen	Pen
Pen		Fountain

As Table 4.1 shows, the same words were not recalled across the three trials. This finding is difficult for decay theory to explain, because it would not predict the recall of a word on trial 3 if it was not recalled on either trial 1 or 2. The fact that some words were recalled on the second and third trials, but not on the first, is difficult for interference theory to explain because it would have to be assumed that what had been unlearned on trial 1 was learned on trial 2 and/or trial 3 (Clifford, 1991). Retrieval-failure theory, however, can explain these findings by arguing that different retrieval cues were in operation across the three trials. Unfortunately, the precise way in which retrieval cues act is not known (Hampson & Morris, 1996).

According to Tulving & Thomson's (1973) *encoding specificity principle*, recall improves if the same cues are present during recall as during the original learning. Tulving (1974) used the term *cue-dependent forgetting* to refer jointly to *context-dependent* and *state-dependent* forgetting. Forgetting is, therefore, a failure of retrieval cues to match the encoded nature of items in memory (Solso, 1995). Environmental or contextual variables represent external cues, whilst psychological or physiological *states* represent *internal cues*.

Abernathy (1940) asked one group of participants to learn and then recall material in the same room, whilst a second group learned material in one room but recalled it in another. Recall was better in the first than second group. Similarly, Godden & Baddeley (1975) had divers learn word lists either on land or 15 feet under water and then tested their recall in either the same or a different context. The results showed a 30 per cent decrement when recall was tested in a different context. They also found that cue-dependent forgetting applies to recall, but not to recognition.

According to Baddeley (1995), large effects of context on memory are only found when the contexts in which encoding and retrieval occur are very different. Although less marked changes can produce some effects, studies (other than Abernathy's) looking at the effects of context on examination performance have *tended* to show few effects. This may be because when we are learning, our surroundings are not a particularly *salient* feature of the situation. However, our internal state is more salient, and can have a powerful effect on recall. Clark *et al.* (1987) have argued that victims' inability to recall details of a violent crime may be due at least in part to the fact that recall occurs in a less emotionally aroused state (see Box 5.4), whilst McCormick & Mayer (1991) have suggested that the important link is between mood and the sort of material being remembered. Thus, we are more likely to remember happy events when we are feeling happy rather than sad.

The permanence of memory

In studies conducted in the 1940s and 50s, Penfield electrically stimulated the cerebral cortex of conscious and alert patients about to undergo brain surgery. Stimulation of certain cortical areas seemed to produce a 'memory' in these patients. Although these 'released memories' were not perfectly detailed, Penfield (1969) concluded that 'each succeeding state of consciousness leaves its permanent imprint on the brain'. Loftus & Loftus (1980) found that 84 per cent of psychologists they surveyed believed that memories were permanently stored, as did 69 per cent of non-psychologists.

However, the evidence from Penfield's studies is not particularly convincing (Eysenck, 1993). For example, of the 520 patients he studied, only 40 reported the recovery of an apparently long-forgotten memory, and those memories that were recovered were typically neither vivid nor detailed.

Conclusions

This chapter has considered several psychological explanations of forgetting. Some of these are better supported by evidence than others. Of those that have survived experimental investigation, some are better applied to forgetting from STM and others to LTM forgetting.

Answers to the tip-of-the-tongue test presented in Box 4.4

1 sampan
2 sextant
3 nepotism
4 cloaca
5 ambergris
6 apse

Summary

- In terms of the multi-store model, **availability** mainly concerns STM and the transfer of information from STM into LTM, whilst **accessibility** mainly concerns LTM.

- According to **motivated-forgetting theory**, memories likely to elicit guilt, embarrassment, shame or anxiety are made inaccessible through the defence mechanism of **repression**.

- Traumatic experiences can produce memory disturbances (as in **psychogenic amnesia**). However Freud's theory has difficulty explaining why psychogenic amnesia sometimes disappears as suddenly as it appeared. Repression may help people experiencing **post-traumatic stress disorder** to cope, but 'repression' does not necessarily imply a strict **Freudian** interpretation.

- **Recovered memories** of child sexual abuse cannot be taken literally because they may relate to pre-verbal early experiences. Repression is not needed to explain 'forgotten' childhood experiences. Similarly, there is experimental evidence for **false memory syndrome**.

- According to the **Gestalt theory of forgetting**, memories become distorted over time in the direction of 'good form'. Apparent empirical support can often be explained in terms of experimental artefacts and biases, and the theory is of little value.

- **Decay/trace decay theory** tries to explain why forgetting increases over time. Some sort of structural change occurs in the brain when learning first occurs (the **engram**) and, unless this is maintained by rehearsal, the memory contained within it will cease to be available.

- Hebb distinguished between an **active trace** (corresponding roughly to STM) and the **structural trace**. Forgetting is caused by disruption of the engram.

- Decay can also explain LTM forgetting, on the assumption that decay occurs through **disuse**. However, certain motor – and other – skills are not lost, even if they are not practised for long periods of time. Neurological decay is not the major cause of LTM forgetting.

- Peterson and Peterson's findings that poorer recall of information occurs with the passage of time appears to support the view that decay occurs in STM. Jenkins and Dallenbach concluded that interference rather than decay is the major cause of LTM forgetting.

- According to **interference theory**, forgetting is influenced more by what we do before or after learning than by the passage of time. In **retroactive interference/inhibition** (RI), later learning prevents the recall of earlier learning (working **backwards**). In **proactive interference/inhibition** (PI), earlier learning prevents recall of later learning (working **forwards**).

- The most important cause of PI may be interference with **retrieval**, as shown by Wickens' participants who became increasingly poor at retaining information in STM on successive trials. But when the **category** of information was changed, participants displayed **release from PI**. This also occurs when people are told about a change of category **either before or after it occurs**, indicating that interference with retrieval rather than storage is the crucial factor.

- Laboratory studies of interference lack **ecological validity**. They tend to use nonsense syllables rather than meaningful material, which is more resistant to interference. Learning to pair words (already part of SM) with nonsense syllables is stored in **episodic memory** (EM), and so interference effects apply mainly to EM. SM is more resistant to interference.

- According to **displacement theory**, in a **limited-capacity** STM system the oldest material is pushed out by incoming new material. Using the **serial-probe task**, Waugh and Norman produced findings consistent with both displacement and decay theories. However, it is unclear whether displacement is distinct from either decay or interference, and may be a combination of the two.

- According to **retrieval-failure theory**, memories cannot be recalled because the correct **retrieval cues** are not being used (as in the **tip-of-the-tongue phenomenon**).

- Tulving's finding that participants free-recalled **different** words on three separate recall trials is better explained by retrieval-failure theory than either decay or interference theories.

- According to the **encoding specificity principle**, recall improves if the same cues are present during recall as during the original learning. **Cue-dependent forgetting** refers jointly to **context-** and **state-dependent forgetting** (relating to environmental/contextual variables and psychological/physiological **states** respectively).

- Large context effects are only found when the encoding and retrieval contexts are very different. During learning, our internal state may be much more **salient**, which might also explain why victims often fail to recall details of a violent crime.

- Penfield's discovery of 'released memories' when electrically stimulating the cortex led him to conclude that memories are permanently stored. However, his evidence is far from convincing and there is no compelling evidence to support the permanent-memory hypothesis.

SOME PRACTICAL APPLICATIONS OF RESEARCH INTO MEMORY

Introduction and overview

5

As interesting as laboratory studies of memory are, they tend to 'minimise many of the features that may be central to our memory in everyday life' (Hampson & Morris, 1996). 'Everyday' things that have been researched include the 'mental maps' of the world we develop through our experiences (e.g. Smith *et al.*, 1994), our memory for medical information (e.g. Ley, 1988), 'prospective memory' (memory for things we *have* to do rather than things we have done: e.g. Morris, 1992), memories across our lifetimes (e.g. Schuman & Rieger, 1992), and our memory for familiar objects such as coins and postage stamps (e.g. Richardson, 1993).

Other areas of interest include eyewitness testimony (e.g. Loftus, 1974), strategies for improving memory (e.g. Higbee, 1996) and memory expertise (e.g. Valentine & Wilding, 1994). This chapter examines research findings concerning these three areas.

Eyewitness testimony

In 1973, the Devlin Committee was established to look at legal cases in England and Wales that had involved an identification parade. Of those people prosecuted after being picked out from an identification parade, 82 per cent were convicted. Of the 347 cases in which prosecution occurred when eyewitness testimony was the *only* evidence against the defendant, 74 per cent were convicted (Devlin, 1976). Although eyewitness testimony is regarded as important evidence in legal cases, the reconstructive nature of memory has led some researchers to question its usefulness (e.g. Fruzzetti *et al.*, 1992; Wells, 1993). Even law-abiding psychologists have been the victims of misidentification.

> **Box 5.1**   *The dangers of being a psychologist interested in eyewitness testimony*
>
> A psychologist in Australia who had appeared in a TV discussion on eyewitness testimony was arrested some time later, picked out in an identity parade by a very distraught woman and told he was being charged with rape. It became clear that the rape had been committed at the time he was taking part in the TV discussion. When the psychologist told the police that he had many witnesses including an Assistant Commissioner of Police, the policeman taking the statement replied: 'Yes, and I suppose you've also got Jesus Christ and the Queen of England too'. It turned out that the woman had been watching the TV programme when the rape occurred and had correctly recognised the face, but not the circumstances.

As noted in Chapter 4, memory may involve fiction as well as fact, due to our tendency to 'fill in the gaps' in our knowledge, or to modify memories so as to match existing schemas. Loftus, the leading researcher in the area of eyewitness testimony, has posed questions like 'Is eyewitness testimony influenced by people's tendency to reconstruct their memories of events to fit their schemas?', 'Can subtle differences in the wording of a question cause witnesses to remember an event differently?' and 'Can witnesses be misled into remembering things that did not actually occur?' Based on numerous studies, Loftus has argued that the evidence given by witnesses in court cases is very unreliable.

Figure 5.1   *Eyewitness testimony may not be as useful as we would like*

The importance of eyewitness testimony, even with a discredited witness

Using a fictitious case, Loftus (1974) asked students to judge the guilt or innocence of a man accused of robbing a grocer's and murdering the owner and his five-year-old granddaughter. On the evidence presented, only nine of the 50 students considered the man to be guilty. Other students were presented with the same case, but were also told that an assistant in the store had testified that the accused was the man who had committed the crimes. This resulted in 36 of the 50 students judging him to be guilty, suggesting that eyewitness testimony does influence juror decisions.

A third group of students was presented with the original evidence and the assistant's eyewitness testimony. However, this group was told that the eyewitness had been *discredited* by the defence lawyer, who had shown that the shortsighted eyewitness was not wearing his glasses when the crime occurred, and could not possibly have seen the face of the accused from his position in the store. Loftus reasoned that if the students were totally fair in their decisions, about the same number would consider the accused to be guilty as occurred in the first group. In fact, 34 of the 50 students judged him to be guilty, suggesting that a mistaken eyewitness is 'better' than no eyewitness at all.

Factors influencing eyewitness testimony

Wells (1993) has reviewed research indicating that several factors concerning suspects are particularly important in influencing the accuracy of eyewitness testimony.

Box 5.2   *Two important factors influencing the accuracy of eyewitnesses*

Race: Errors are more likely to occur when the suspect's race differs from that of the witness (Brigham & Malpass, 1985). Luce (1974), for example, found that African American, white American and Chinese American participants recognised members of their own race

---

extremely well. However, participants of *all* races were significantly poorer at recognising faces of people of other races. This is reflected in the comment that 'They all look the same to me' when referring to members of different races (the *illusion of outgroup homogeneity*).

Clothing: According to Sanders (1984), witnesses pay more attention to a suspect's clothing than to more stable characteristics such as height and facial features. In Sanders' experiment, participants saw a video of a crime in which the criminal wore glasses and a T-shirt. Afterwards, they were asked to select the criminal in an identification parade and were more likely to select a person wearing glasses and a T-shirt. Evidently, criminals are aware of this, since they change their appearance prior to an identity parade (Brigham & Malpass, 1985).

The effects of 'leading questions' on eyewitness testimony

According to Loftus, it is the form of questions that witnesses are asked which mainly influences how they 'remember' what they 'witnessed'. 'Leading questions' are interesting because they can introduce new information which may alter a witness's memory of an event. By either their *form* or *content*, such questions can suggest to a witness the answer that *should* be given. Lawyers are skilled at deliberately asking such questions, and the police may also use such questioning when interrogating suspects and witnesses to a crime.

Loftus & Palmer (1974) tested the effect of changing a single word in certain critical questions on the judgement of speed. Participants were shown a 30-second videotape of two cars colliding, and were then asked several questions about the collision. One group was asked 'About how fast were the cars going when they hit?'. For others, the word 'hit' was replaced by *smashed, collided, bumped* or *contacted*. These words have very different connotations regarding the speed and force of impact, and this was reflected in the judgements given. Those who heard the word 'hit' produced an average speed estimate of 34.0 mph. For 'smashed', 'collided', 'bumped' and 'contacted', the average estimates were 40.8 mph, 39.3 mph, 38.1 mph, and 31.8 mph respectively.

Figure 5.2 *Assessments of speed of crashing vehicles can be influenced by the verb used to describe the impact. While (a) represents 'two cars hitting', (b) represents 'two cars smashing'. Which word is used in a question about speed can influence people's estimates of how fast the cars were travelling at the time of impact*

Loftus and Palmer wanted to know if memory itself undergoes change as a result of misleading questions or whether the existing memorial representation of the accident is merely being supplemented by misleading questions. *Memory as reconstruction* implies that memory itself is transformed at the time of retrieval, that is, what was originally encoded changes when it is recalled.

This was tested in a follow-up experiment in which those participants who had heard the words 'smashed' and 'hit' returned to the laboratory one week later. Without seeing the film again, the participants were asked questions, one of which was whether they remembered seeing *any broken glass* (even though there was none in the film). If 'smashed' really had influenced participants' memories of the accident as being more serious than it was, then they might also 'remember' details they did not actually see, but which are consistent with an accident occurring at high speed (such as broken glass).

Of the 50 participants asked about the 'smashing' cars, 16 (32 per cent) reported that they had seen broken glass. Only seven (14 per cent) of the 50 asked about the 'hitting' cars reported seeing broken glass. This suggests that the answer to the question about the glass was determined by the earlier question about speed, which had changed what was originally encoded when seeing the film.

Box 5.3   *The effects on memory of 'after-the-fact' information (Loftus, 1975)*

Participants witnessed a short videotape of a car travelling through the countryside. Half were asked 'How fast was the white sports car going while travelling along the country road?' The other half were asked 'How fast was the car going when it passed the barn while travelling along the country road?' The second question, of course, *presupposes* that the car actually passed a barn. In fact, it didn't. A week later, participants were again questioned about what they had seen. Of those who had previously answered the question pre-supposing there was a barn on the videotape, 17.3 per cent answered 'yes' to the question 'Did you see a barn?'. Only 2.7 per cent of the other participants claimed to have seen one.

Loftus argues that leading questions not only produce biased answers, but actually distort memory. Loftus & Zanni (1975) showed participants a short film depicting a car accident, after which each participant answered questions about what they had witnessed. Some were asked whether they had seen *a* broken headlight, whilst others were asked whether they had seen *the* broken headlight. The results showed that those asked about *the* headlight were far more likely to report having seen one than those asked about *a* headlight.

The same effect has been obtained in non-laboratory settings. For example, Loftus (1979) staged a fake crime at a busy train station. Two of Loftus's female students left a large bag unattended on a bench, and while they were gone, a male student reached inside the bag, pretended to pull out an object and place it under his coat before walking away. When the women returned, one cried out: 'Oh my God, my tape recorder is missing!'. They then began to talk to potential eyewitnesses, most of whom agreed to give them their phone number in case their testimony was needed.

A week later, a student posing as an 'insurance agent' phoned the witnesses and asked them to recall details about the incident. The questioning ended with the witness being asked 'Did you see the tape recorder?'. Although there was no tape recorder, more than half of the eyewitnesses 'remembered' seeing it, and most were able to give 'details' about it such as its colour, shape and even the height of the aerial. Most also claimed that they would be able to recognise the thief again.

Using a staged event with five- and seven-year-old children, Memon & Vartoukian (1996) found that recall improved on repeated questioning using open questions. However, accuracy tended to deteriorate upon repetition of closed questions (requiring a 'yes' or 'no' answer). The use of repeated, closed questions may lead witnesses to conclude, incorrectly, that their initial response was incorrect, which may have an adverse effect on accuracy.

Loftus believes that her findings are disturbing, particularly when viewed in the light of what often happens to eyewitnesses questioned by the police, who may introduce incorrect information by asking leading questions. The answer to the question 'are eyewitnesses reliable?' is, therefore, 'sometimes' at best, and 'no' at worst (Loftus, 1979).

An evaluation of Loftus's research

According to Tversky and Tuchin (1989):

'there is now substantial support for the view that misleading information affects memory for the original information'.

However, Bekerian & Bowers (1983) have argued that if witnesses are asked questions that follow the order of events in strict sequence, rather than being asked in Loftus's relatively unstructured way, they are *not* influenced by the bias introduced by subsequent questions. For Baddeley (1995), the 'Loftus effect' is *not* due to the destruction of the memory trace. Rather, it is due to interfering with its *retrieval*.

McCloskey & Zaragoza (1985) have challenged the claim that eyewitnesses are mainly unreliable. Loftus herself has acknowledged that when misleading information is 'blatantly incorrect', it has no effects on a witness's memory. For example, Loftus (1979) showed participants colour slides of a man stealing a red purse from a woman's bag. Ninety-eight per cent of those who saw the slides correctly identified the purse's colour, and when they read a description of the event which referred to a 'brown purse', all but two continued to remember it as red.

This suggests that our memory for obviously important information accurately perceived at the time is not easily distorted, a finding confirmed in studies where people have witnessed a real (and violent) crime (Yuille & Cutshall, 1986). People are more likely to be misled if the false information they are given concerns *insignificant* details peripheral to the main event, if the false information is given after a delay (when the memory of the event has had time to fade), and if they have no reason to distrust it (Cohen, 1993).

Cognitive interviews

To elicit accurate and detailed information from eyewitnesses, an increasing number of police forces are using the *cognitive interview technique* (Geiselman, 1988). This draws on Tulving's research concerning the relationship between encoding and retrieval (see Chapter 4, page 78).

Box 5.4 *The four procedures of the cognitive interview technique*

1 **Reinstating the context:** This involves the interviewer and interviewee attempting to recreate the context (the surrounding environment, such as the temperature and the witness's own state) in which the incident occurred, before any attempt is made to recall what happened.

2 **Reporting the event:** Once the context has been recreated, the witness is required to report any information he or she can remember, even if it is not considered important.

> **3 Recalling the event in a different order:** The third step is for the witness to try to recall the events in, say, the reverse order or by starting from whatever was most memorable about the event.
> **4 Changing perspectives:** Finally, the witness is asked to try to recall the event from, say, the perspective of a prominent figure in the event (such as the cashier in the case of a bank robbery), and to think about what the cashier must have seen.
> **(Adapted from Hampson & Morris, 1996)**

Geiselman has shown that the cognitive interview technique produces significantly better recall than the usual interview techniques used by the police, a finding also obtained by other researchers (e.g. Roy, 1991).

Despite continued debate about eyewitness testimony, there is little doubt that Loftus and others have shown that our knowledge of the processes involved in memory can be usefully applied in the 'real world'. The Devlin Committee's report (see page 85), for example, recommended that the trial judge be required to instruct the jury that it is not safe to convict on a single eyewitness testimony alone, unless (a) the circumstances are exceptional (such as the witness being a close friend or relative), or (b) when there is substantial corroborative evidence. The Devlin Committee's safeguards are much stronger than those of the US supreme court, but similar to those of American legal experts.

Improving memory

Mnemonics

Techniques for aiding recall, which most people consider unusual and artificial, are called *mnemonics*. According to Belezza (1981), mnemonics have two fundamental characteristics. First, they are not inherently connected to the material that has to be learned, but impose meaning and structure on material that is otherwise not very meaningful and structured. Second, they typically involve adding something to the material to create meaningful associations between what is to be learned and what is already stored in LTM.

Rather than simplifying information, mnemonic devices make it more elaborate, resulting in *more*, rather than less, information being stored in memory. However, the additional information makes the material easier to recall, organising it into a cohesive whole so that retrieval of part of the information ensures retrieval of the rest.

Snowman *et al.* (1980) taught college students on a 'study skills' course to use the *method of loci* (see page 45) to remember the central concepts from a 2200-word passage of prose. Compared with students taught more traditional study skills, the group that used the loci method recalled significantly more ideas from the passage. The method of loci has also been used successfully by special populations such as the blind, brain damaged and elderly (Yesavage & Rose, 1984).

In the seventeenth century, Herdson used a device which involves imagining numbers as objects (Hunter, 1957). For example, 1 might be imagined as a pencil, 2 as a swan and so on. The items to be remembered are then imagined interacting with their relevant number. For example, if the first item to be remembered were 'clock', an image of a clock with a pencil for the minute hand might be formed.

Higbee (1996) has distinguished between visual mnemonic *systems* (using imagery) and verbal mnemonic *techniques*, which make associations with words. Verbal mnemonics include *rhymes* ('In fourteen hundred and ninety-two, Columbus sailed the ocean blue'), *acrostics* (a verse in which the first letters correspond with the material that needs to be remembered, as in 'Richard Of York Gave Battle In Vain' for the colours of the rainbow), *acronyms* (such as HOMES for the five great lakes: Huron, Ontario, Michigan, Erie and Superior) and *association* ('my PAL the princiPAL', to distinguish its spelling from 'principLE as a ruLE').

Other mnemonic *methods* (neither 'systems' nor 'techniques') consist of both a verbal and a visual process, such as the *key-* or *peg-word system* introduced to England in the late nineteenth century by Sambrook (Paivio, 1979). In this, a rhyme such as 'one is a bun, two is a shoe, three is a tree' and so on is used to associate an object (the key or peg word) with each number in the rhyme. The items to be remembered are then individually paired with a key word by means of a mental image. For example, if the first word to be remembered is 'clock', an image of a bun with a clock face might be formed. For each of the items, the rhyme is recited and the mental image previously formed is 'triggered', resulting in the item's recall.

Box 5.5 *The link-word method*

A variation on the key- or peg-word method is the *link-word method*. First systematically studied by Atkinson (1975), it has been used extensively in the teaching of foreign languages (e.g. Gruneberg, 1992). It involves initially constructing a concrete link word or words to represent the foreign word to be learned. For example, the Greek word for 'worm' is 'skooleekee'. This could be represented by two words which sound similar to 'skooleekee', namely 'school' and 'leaky'. Next, a verbal image is formed connecting the link word or words with its English meaning. For example, the learner could picture his or her school leaky and worms falling through the roof. Once the image has been formed, which involves the learner thinking very hard about it for at least ten seconds, the meaning of the Greek word can be obtained by retrieving the link words 'school' and 'leaky' and then the stored image that links these words to 'worm'.

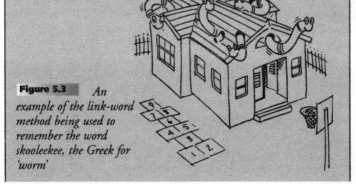

Figure 5.3 *An example of the link-word method being used to remember the word skooleekee, the Greek for 'worm'*

The link-word method is highly effective for foreign language learning (Young, 1971), and has also been successfully used by medical students. Bower (1973) gives an example of a method by which the twelve cranial nerves can be stored:

'At the oil factory (*olfactory* nerve), the optician (*optic*) looked for the occupant (*oculomotor*) of the truck (*trochlear*). He was searching because three gems (*trigeminal*) had been abducted (*abducens*) by a man who was hiding his face (*facial*) and ears (*auditory*). A glossy photograph (*glossopharyngeal*) had been taken of him, but it was too vague (*vagus*) to use. He also appeared to be spineless (*spinal accessory*) and hypocritical (*hypoglossal*)'.

Other approaches to memory improvement

Several studies have shown that it is easier to recall an event or experience if we are in the same location or context in which the information was first encoded (Estes, 1972: see Chapter 4). This suggests that if we learn material in a particular place, the best way of trying to recall it would be to go to the same place (revising in the examination hall in roughly the position you would expect to be sitting in the examination, perhaps?). Consistent with Abernathy's (1940) results (see page 79), students appear to perform better if tested in the room in which they were taught (Wingfield, 1979), and it may even be helpful to imagine that we are in that place when we try to recall information (Smith, 1979).

As seen in Chapter 4, our *internal state* (emotions or physiological condition) can act as a context which influences recall. For example, some studies have shown that when people encode material under the influence of drugs like alcohol and marijuana, recall is better when the intoxicated state is re-created compared with recall in a non-intoxicated state. Similarly, some studies have shown that people remember things better when they are in the same mood or emotional state as when the information was encoded (e.g. Eich & Metcalfe, 1989), although others have found little evidence of this (e.g. Bower & Mayer, 1985).

Study skills

Many textbooks (including this one) offer an introduction and overview to each chapter and a summary of the material. Reder & Anderson (1980) found that of two groups of students who spent the same amount of time studying, those who read only the summary remembered more than those who read the whole text. This was true when questions were taken directly from the text or required the combination of material and the drawing of inferences! Moreover, the difference was maintained even when the main points to be remembered were underlined for the students reading the whole text. Clearly, we would not wish to advocate reading only the summaries of each chapter in this book, but Reder and Anderson's findings suggest that summaries can be useful as revision aids.

Study guides designed to help the reader retain as much information as possible from a book include Thomas & Robinson's (1972) *PQ4R method*. In this, the reader begins by **p**reviewing the material to familiarise him/herself with the range of topics a chapter covers. Next, the reader prepares **q**uestions that focus on key concepts and issues. With these questions in mind, the chapter is then **r**ead, with time being taken to **r**eflect on the meaning of the information and its relation to what is already known. Once the chapter has been read, the reader **r**ecites what has been read, using the questions as reminders (with those parts that are difficult being re-read). Finally, the entire material is **r**eviewed in the reader's mind, again using questions to structure this task.

Box 5.6 *Practical strategies for maximising learning*

- **Reduce the material to a manageable amount:** It is unlikely that every single point in a chapter is important. Therefore, try to reduce the material to its salient points.
- **Impose meaning on the material:** *Elaborative rehearsal* is much more effective than maintenance rehearsal in producing

---

retention (see Chapter 2). An example would be making something you have read about relevant to your own experiences.

- **Learn the whole:** Recall tends to be better if material is reviewed as a whole rather than being broken into smaller parts. Only when material is particularly long and complicated is breaking it up effective.

- **Use periodic retrieval:** Instead of passively reading and re-reading material, engage in periodic retrieval to determine if the material has been effectively encoded. If it has not, review the material again.

- **Engage in overlearning:** Ebbinghaus (see Chapter 1, page 2) found that he could improve his retention of material by repeatedly reviewing it after he had reached 100 per cent accuracy. Once something has been mastered, it should be reviewed at least once or twice.

- **Use study breaks and rewards:** We can only function so long at maximum efficiency before our concentration begins to wane. Taking a break every so often, and doing something rewarding in between, allows us to return to work refreshed.

- **Space study sessions:** Two three-hour or three two-hour study sessions usually result in better retention than a single six-hour session.

- **Avoid interference:** Competing material produces interference effects. If you have to work on two or more subjects in the same time frame, try to make them as dissimilar as possible to reduce proactive and retroactive interference (see Chapter 4, page 70). Planning study sessions to avoid this possibility is obviously helpful.

- **Use time effectively:** Try to develop a time management schedule (incorporating spaced study sessions) in which certain times are devoted to study and certain others to leisure. Once the schedule has been constructed, stick to it!

(Based on Crooks & Stein, 1991)

Understanding memory expertise

People with 'supernormal' memories have long been of interest to both the general public and professional psychologists. Wilding & Valentine (1994) have made a special study of memory expertise, drawing on (amongst other sources) the World Memory Championships (or 'Memoriad'), first staged in 1991. The feats of some of the competitors are truly astonishing. For example, Hideaki Tomoyori recited 40,000 digits of pi in 17 hours and 21 minutes (including 255 minutes for breaks!), whilst the 1993 winner could recall the correct order of 416 playing cards (or eight complete packs).

Valentine & Wilding (1994) have shown that outstanding performers can be divided into *strategists*, who use particular methods to store information (such as the mnemonic techniques described above) and *naturals*, who do not (and appear to have a yet-to-be-understood 'natural ability'). The former tend to perform better on 'strategic' tasks, such as face recognition and word recall, whilst the latter tend to perform better on 'non-strategic' tasks, such as recognising snow crystals and the temporal order of pictures.

Whilst Valentine and Wilding have also found that some people appear to have a superior memory across a wide range of tasks, other research indicates that in some 'strategists' performance is confined to tasks for which their methods are best suited (Biederman *et al.*, 1992). Valentine and Wilding believe that the principles employed by strategic memorisers are those on which normal memory processes are based, namely *semanticisation* (making the meaningless meaningful), *imagery* and *association*. Strategists, however, use these methods in a conscious and intentional way.

Whilst the study of naturally good memory is very recent, Valentine and Wilding believe that progress can be made by looking at the development of natural memory and the possibility of a critical period for its development, the relationship between memory and cognitive abilities such as intelligence, and the neurophysiological and biochemical bases of natural memory.

Conclusions

This chapter has looked at some of the ways in which our knowledge of human memory has been applied practically, and has identified important insights into 'everyday' memory. Although such research has been criticised for using methodologies which fall short of those employed in laboratory studies of memory (e.g. Banaji & Crowder, 1989), a 'balance sheet' on the advantages and disadvantages of research into the practical applications of memory research seems to show it to be very much in the black (Eysenck & Keane, 1995).

Summary

- Three aspects of everyday memory which have been researched are eyewitness testimony, strategies for improving memory and memory expertise.
- The Devlin Committee found that even when identification parades were the **only** evidence against the defendant, conviction rates were very high. This is worrying given memory's reconstructive nature and known miscarriages of justice resulting from eyewitness testimony.
- According to Loftus, the evidence given by witnesses in court cases can be highly unreliable. A **discredited** eyewitness may influence jurors to almost the same extent as a non-discredited witness.
- The accuracy of eyewitness testimony is influenced by the suspect's **race** (reflecting the **illusion of outgroup homogeneity**) and **clothing** (which is more influential than height or facial features).
- Loftus believes that **leading questions** are especially important, because they can introduce new information which can alter memory of the event. **Memory as reconstruction** implies that memory, at the time of retrieval, undergoes change as a result of misleading questions. 'After-the-fact' information can also change memory for an event.

- The 'Loftus effect' may be due to interference with the retrieval of the memory trace, not to its destruction. If witnesses are asked questions that follow the sequence of events, rather than in Loftus's unstructured way, they are **not** influenced by the bias introduced by subsequent questions.

- Loftus herself has demonstrated that memory for obviously **significant** details which are accurately perceived at the time is not easily distorted. People are more likely to be misled if the false information concerns insignificant details, is delayed, and if they have no reason to believe they are being misinformed.

- Increasingly, police forces are using Geiselman's **cognitive interview technique,** which involves **reinstating the context**, **reporting the event**, **recalling the event in a different order** and **changing perspectives**. This technique produces significantly better recall than traditional police interviews.

- **Mnemonics** are not inherently connected to the material that has to be learned, but impose meaning and structure on relatively meaningless or unstructured material. They also involve adding something to the material by way of meaningful associations with what is already stored in LTM.

- Visual mnemonic **systems** use imagery, whilst verbal mnemonic techniques (such as **rhymes**, **acrostics**, **acronyms** and **association**) use word associations. Other methods combine verbal and visual components, such as the **key-** or **peg-word system** and the related **link-word method** (widely used in foreign language teaching and by medical students).

- It is easier to recall something in the same **context** in which it was originally encoded. **Internal state**, such as being under the influence of drugs, can act as a context influencing recall, but the evidence is inconclusive, as it is in relation to mood or emotional state.

- Many textbooks include an introduction and overview to each chapter, plus a summary of the chapter content, as aids to learning. Reder and Anderson found that reading just the chapter summaries can be more useful than reading the whole text.

- A popular form of study guide is the **PQ4R method**. Other practical strategies for maximising learning include: reducing the material to a manageable amount, imposing meaning on the material (elaborative rehearsal), learning the whole, periodic retrieval, overlearning, using study breaks and rewards, spacing study sessions, avoiding interference, and using time effectively.

- Valentine and Wilding have studied the feats of people with supernormal memories. They divide outstanding performers into **strategists** and **naturals**. The former use **semanticisation**, **imagery** and **association**, the basic principles of normal memory processes. Less is known about the strategies used by naturals.

REFERENCES

ABERNATHY, E.M. (1940) The effect of changed environmental conditions upon the results of college examinations. *Journal of Psychology*, 10, 293–301.

ALBA, J.W. & HASHER, L. (1983) Is memory schematic? *Psychological Bulletin*, 93, 203–231.

ALLPORT, G.W. & POSTMAN, L. (1947) *The Psychology of Rumour*. New York: Holt, Rinehart & Winston.

ANDERSON, J.R. (1983) *The Architecture of Cognition* (2nd edition). Cambridge, MA: Harvard University Press.

ANDERSON, J.R. (1995) *Cognitive Psychology and its Implications*. New York: W.H. Freeman & Company.

ATKINSON, R.C. (1975) Mnemonotechnics in second-language learning. *American Psychologist*, 30, 821–828.

ATKINSON, R.C. & SHIFFRIN, R.M. (1968) Human memory: A proposed system and its control processes. In K.W. Spence & J.T. Spence (Eds) *The Psychology of Learning and Motivation*, Volume 2. London: Academic Press.

ATKINSON, R.C. & SHIFFRIN, R.M. (1971) The control of short-term memory. *Scientific American*, 224, 82–90.

BADDELEY, A.D. (1966) The influence of acoustic and semantic similarity on long-term memory for word sequences. *Quarterly Journal of Experimental Psychology*, 18, 302–309.

BADDELEY, A.D. (1968) Closure and response bias in short-term memory for form. *British Journal of Psychology*, 59, 139–145.

BADDELEY, A.D. (1976) *The Psychology of Memory*. New York: Basic Books.

BADDELEY, A.D. (1981) The concept of working memory: A view of its current state and probable future development. *Cognition*, 10, 17–23.

BADDELEY, A.D. (1986) *Working Memory*. Oxford: Oxford University Press.

BADDELEY, A.D. (1990) *Human Memory*. Hove: Lawrence Erlbaum Associates.

BADDELEY, A.D. (1995) Memory. In C.C. French & A.M. Colman (Eds) *Cognitive Psychology*. London: Longman.

BADDELEY, A.D. & HITCH, G. (1974) Working memory. In G.H. Bower (Ed.) *Recent Advances in Learning and Motivation*, Volume 8. New York: Academic Press.

BADDELEY, A.D. & SCOTT, D. (1971) Short-term forgetting in the absence of proactive inhibition. *Quarterly Journal of Experimental Psychology*, 23, 275–283.

BADDELEY, A.D., THOMSON, N. & BUCHANAN, M. (1975) Word length and the structure of short-term memory. *Journal of Verbal Learning and Verbal Behaviour*, 14, 575–589.

BAHRICK, H.P. (1984) Semantic memory content in permastore: Fifty years of memory for Spanish learned in school. *Journal of Experimental Psychology: General*, 113, 1–29.

BAHRICK, H.P. & HALL, L.K. (1991) Lifetime maintenance of high-school mathematics content. *Journal of Experimental Psychology: General*, 120, 20–33.

BANAJI, M.R. & CROWDER, R.G. (1989) The bankruptcy of everyday memory. *American Psychologist*, 44, 1185–1193.

BARON, R.A. (1989) *Psychology: The Essential Science*. London: Allyn & Bacon.

BARTLETT, F.C. (1932) *Remembering*. Cambridge: Cambridge University Press.

BEKERIAN, D.A. & BOWERS, J.M. (1983) Eye-witness testimony: Were we misled? *Journal of Experimental Psychology: Learning, Memory and Cognition*, 9, 139–145.

BELEZZA, F.S. (1981) Mnemonic devices: Classification, characteristics and criteria. *Review of Educational Research*, 51, 247–275.

BIEDERMAN, I., COOPER, E.E., MAHDEVAN, R.S. & FOX, P.W. (1992) Unexceptional spatial memory in an exceptional mnemonist. *Journal of Experimental Psychology: Learning, Memory and Cognition*, 18, 654–657.

BLAKEMORE, C. (1988) *The Mind Machine*. London: BBC Publications.

BOUSFIELD, W.A. (1953) The occurrence of clustering in the recall of randomly arranged associates. *Journal of General Psychology*, 49, 229–240.

BOWER, G.H. (1972) Mental imagery and associative learning. In L. Gregg (Ed.) *Cognition in Learning and Memory*. New York: Wiley.

BOWER, G.H. (1973) How to … uh … remember! *Psychology Today*, October, 63–70.

BOWER, G.H., BLACK, J.B. & TURNER, T.J. (1979) Scripts in memory for text. *Cognitive Psychology*, 11, 177–220.

BOWER, G.H. & CLARK, M.C. (1969) Narrative stories as mediators for serial learning. *Psychonomic Science*, 14, 181–182.

BOWER, G.H., CLARK, M.C., LESGOLD, A. & WINSENZ, D. (1969) Hierarchical retrieval schemes in recall of categorised word lists. *Journal of Verbal Learning and Verbal Behaviour*, 8, 323–343.

BOWER, G.H. & HILGARD, E.R. (1981) *Theories of Learning*. Englewood Cliffs, NJ: Prentice Hall.

BOWER, G.H. & MAYER, J. (1985) Failure to replicate mood-dependent retrieval. *Bulletin of the Psychonomic Society*, 23, 39–42.

BOWER, G.H. & SPRINGSTON, F. (1970) Pauses as recoding points in letter series. *Journal of Experimental Psychology*, 83, 421–430.

BRANSFORD, J.D., FRANKS, J.J., MORRIS, C.D. & STEIN, B.S. (1979) Some general constraints on learning and memory research. In L.S. Cermak & F.I.M. Craik (Eds) *Levels of Processing in Human Memory*. Hillsdale, NJ: Erlbaum.

BRANSFORD, J.D. & JOHNSON, M.K. (1972) Contextual prerequisites for understanding: Some investigations of comprehension and recall. *Journal of Verbal Learning and Verbal Behaviour*, 11, 717–726.

BRIGHAM, J. & MALPASS, R.S. (1985) The role of experience and contact in the recognition of faces of own- and other-race persons. *Journal of Social Issues*, 41, 139–155.

BRITISH PSYCHOLOGICAL SOCIETY (1995) *Recovered Memories: The Report of the Working Party of the British Psychological Society*. Leicester: British Psychological Society.

BROADBENT, D.E., COOPER, P.J. & BROADBENT, M.H.P. (1978) A comparison of hierarchical and matrix retrieval schemes in recall. *Journal of Experimental Psychology: Human Learning and Memory*, 4, 486–497.

BROWN, J.A. (1958) Some tests of the decay theory of immediate memory. *Quarterly Journal of Experimental Psychology*, 10, 12–21.

BROWN, R. & KULIK, J. (1977) Flashbulb memories. *Cognition*, 5, 73–99.

BROWN, R. & KULIK, J. (1982) Flashbulb memories. In U. Neisser (Ed.) *Memory Observed*. San Francisco: Freeman.

BROWN, R. & McNEILL, D. (1966) The 'tip-of-the-tongue' phenomenon. *Journal of Verbal Learning and Verbal Behaviour*, 5, 325–337.

CARLSON, N.R. (1987) *Discovering Psychology*. London: Allyn & Bacon.

CHANDLER, C. (1989) Specific retroactive interference in modified recognition tests: Evidence for an unknown cause of interference. *Journal of Experimental Psychology: Learning, Memory and Cognition*, 15, 256–265.

CLARK, M.S., MILLBERG, S. & ERBER, R. (1987) Arousal and state dependent memory: Evidence and some implications for understanding social judgements and social behaviour. In K. Fiedler & J.P. Forgas (Eds) *Affect, Cognition and Social Behaviour*. Toronto: Hogrefe.

CLIFFORD, B. (1980) Recent developments in memory. In J. Radford & E. Govier (Eds) *A Textbook of Psychology*. London: Sheldon.

CLIFFORD, B. (1991) Memory. In J. Radford & E. Govier (Eds) *A Textbook of Psychology* (2nd edition). London: Routledge.

COHEN, G. (1990) Memory. In I. Roth (Ed.) *Introduction to Psychology*, Volume 2. Milton Keynes: Open University Press.

COHEN, G. (1993) Everyday memory and memory systems: The experimental approach. In G. Cohen, G. Kiss & M. Levoi (Eds) *Memory: Current Issues* (2nd edition). Buckingham: Open University Press.

COLLINS, A.M. & LOFTUS, E.F. (1975) A spreading-activation theory of semantic processing. *Psychological Review*, 82, 407–428.

COLLINS, A.M. & QUILLIAN, M.R. (1969) *Retrieval time for semantic memory. Journal of Verbal Learning and Verbal Behaviour*, 8, 240–247.

COLLINS, A.M. & QUILLIAN, M.R. (1972) How to make a language user. In E. Tulving & W. Donaldson (Eds) *Organisation of Memory*. New York: Academic Press.

CONRAD, C. (1972) Cognitive economy in semantic memory. *Journal of Experimental Psychology*, 92, 148–154.

CONRAD, R. (1964) Acoustic confusion in immediate memory. *British Journal of Psychology*, 55, 75–84.

CONWAY, M.A., ANDERSON, S.J., LARSEN, S.F., DONNELLY, C.M., McDANIEL, M.A., McCLELLAND, A.G.R. & RAWLES, R.E. (1994). The formation of flashbulb memories. *Memory and Cognition*, 22, 326–343.

COWAN, N. (1984) On short and long auditory stores. *Psychological Bulletin*, 96, 341–370.

CRAIK, F.I.M. & LOCKHART, R. (1972) Levels of processing. *Journal of Verbal Learning and Verbal Behaviour*, 11, 671–684.

CRAIK, F.I.M. & TULVING, E. (1975) Depth of processing and retention of words in episodic memory. *Journal of Experimental Psychology: General*, 104, 268–294.

CRAIK, F.I.M. & WATKINS, M.J. (1973) The role of rehearsal in short-term memory. *Journal of Verbal Learning and Verbal Behaviour*, 12, 599–607.

CROOKS, R.L. & STEIN, J. (1991) *Psychology: Science, Behaviour and Life* (2nd edition). London: Holt, Rinehart & Winston Inc.

DARWIN, C.J., TURVEY, M.T. & CROWDER, R.G. (1972) An auditory analogue of the Sperling partial report procedure: Evidence for brief auditory storage. *Cognitive Psychology*, 3, 225–267.

DE GROOT, A.D. (1966) Perception and memory versus thought: Some old ideas and recent findings. In B. Kleinmuntz (Ed.) *Problem-Solving: Research, Method and Theory*. New York: Wiley.

DEVLIN REPORT (1976) Report to the Secretary of State for the Home Development of the Departmental Committee on Evidence of Identification in Criminal Cases. London: HMSO.

EBBINGHAUS, H. (1885) *On Memory*. Leipzig: Duncker.

EICH, E. & METCALFE, J. (1989) Mood-dependent memory for internal versus external events. *Journal of Experimental Psychology: Learning, Memory and Cognition*, 15, 443–455.

ESTES, W.K. (1972) An associative basis for coding and organisation in memory. In A. Melton & E. Martin (Eds) *Coding Processes in Human Memory*. Washington, DC: Winston.

EYSENCK, M.W. (1986) Working memory. In G. Cohen, M.W. Eysenck & M.A. Le Voi (Eds) *Memory: A Cognitive Approach*. Milton Keynes: Open University Press.

EYSENCK, M.W. (1993) *Principles of Cognitive Psychology*. Hove: Erlbaum.

EYSENCK, M.W. & EYSENCK, M.C. (1980) Effects of processing depth, distinctiveness and word frequency on retention. *British Journal of Psychology*, 71, 263–274.

EYSENCK, M.W. & KEANE, M.J. (1995) *Cognitive Psychology: A Student's Handbook* (3rd edition). Hove: Erlbaum.

FREUD, S. (1901) The psychopathology of everyday life. In J. Strachey (Ed.) *The Standard Edition of the Complete Works of Sigmund Freud*, Volume 6. London: Hogarth Press.

FRUZZETTI, A.E., TOLAND, K., TELLER, S.A. & LOFTUS, E.F. (1992) Memory and eyewitness testimony. In M. Gruneberg & P.E. Morris (Eds) *Aspects of Memory: The Practical Aspects*. London: Routledge.

GABRIELI, J.D.E., COHEN, N.J. & CORKIN, S. (1988) The impaired learning of semantic knowledge following bilateral medial temporal lobe resection. *Brain*, 7, 157–177.

GARDINER, J.M., CRAIK, F.I.M. & BIRTWISTLE, J. (1972) Retrieval cues and release from proactive inhibition. *Journal of Verbal Learning and Verbal Behaviour*, 11, 778–783.

GATHERCOLE, S.E. & BADDELEY, A.D. (1990) Phonological memory deficits in language-disordered children: Is there a causal connection? *Journal of Memory and Language*, 29, 336–360.

GEISELMAN, R.E. (1988) Improving eyewitness memory through mental reinstatement of context. In G.M. Davies & D.M. Thomson (Eds) *Memory in Context: Context in Memory*. Chichester: Wiley.

GILHOOLY, K. (1996) Working memory and thinking. *The Psychologist*, 9, 82.

GLANZER, M. & CUNITZ, A.R. (1966) Two storage mechanisms in free recall. *Journal of Verbal Learning and Verbal Behaviour*, 5, 928–935.

GLANZER, M. & MEINZER, A. (1967) The effects of intralist activity on free recall. *Journal of Verbal Learning and Verbal Behaviour*, 6, 928–935.

GODDEN, D. & BADDELEY, A.D. (1975) Context-dependent memory in two natural environments: On land and under water. *British Journal of Psychology*, 66, 325–331.

GROSS, R. & McILVEEN, R. (1997) *Cognitive Psychology*. London: Hodder & Stoughton.

GROSS, R. & McILVEEN, R. (1998) *Psychology: A New Introduction*. London: Hodder & Stoughton.

GRUNEBERG, M. (1992) *Linkword Language System: Greek*. London: Corgi Books.

GUNTER, B., CLIFFORD, B. & BERRY, C. (1980) Release from proactive interference with television news items: Evidence for encoding dimensions within televised news. *Journal of Experimental Psychology*: Human Learning and Memory, 6, 216–223.

HABER, R.N. (1969) Eidetic images. *Scientific American*, 220, 36–44.

HABER, R.N. (1980) Eidetic images are not just imaginary. *Psychology Today*, November, 72–82.

HAMPSON, P.J. & MORRIS, P.E. (1996) *Understanding Cognition*. Oxford: Blackwell.

HAMPTON, J.A. (1979) Polymorphous concepts in semantic memory. *Journal of Verbal Learning and Verbal Behaviour*, 18, 441–461.

HART, J., BERNDT, R.S. & CARAMAZZA, A. (1985) Category-specific naming deficit following cerebral infarction. *Nature*, 316, 439–440.

HASSETT, J. & WHITE, M. (1989) *Psychology in Perspective* (2nd edition). Cambridge: Harper & Row.

HEBB, D.O. (1949) *The Organisation of Behaviour*. New York: Wiley.

HIGBEE, K.L. (1996) *Your Memory: How it Works and How to Improve it*. New York: Marlowe and Co.

HIGHFIELD, R. (1997) Forgetfulness opens windows on the mind. *The Daily Telegraph*, 18 July, 3.

HOUSTON, J.P., HAMMEN, C., PADILLA, A. & BEE, H. (1991) *Invitation to Psychology* (3rd ed.). London: Harcourt Brace Jovanovitch.

HUNTER, I.M.L. (1957) *Memory, Facts and Fallacies*. Harmondsworth: Penguin.

HYDE, T.S. & JENKINS, J.J. (1973) Recall for words as a function of semantic, graphic and syntactic orienting tasks. *Journal of Verbal Learning and Verbal Behaviour*, 12, 471–480.

IRWIN, F.W. & SEIDENFELD, M.A. (1937) The application of the method of comparison to the problem of memory change. *Journal of Experimental Psychology*, 21, 363–381.

JAMES, H. (1958) Guessing, expectancy and autonomous change. *Quarterly Journal of Experimental Psychology*, 10, 107–110.

JAMES, W. (1890) *The Principles of Psychology*. New York: Henry Holt & Company.

JENKINS, J.G. & DALLENBACH, K.M. (1924) Oblivescence during sleep and waking. *American Journal of Psychology*, 35, 605–612.

JOHNSON-LAIRD, P.N., HERRMAN, D.J. & CHAFFIN, R. (1984) Only connections: A critique of semantic networks. *Psychological Bulletin*, 96, 292–315.

JONES, W. & ANDERSON, J. (1987) Short- and long-term memory retrieval: A comparison of the effects of information load and relatedness. *Journal of Experimental Psychology: General*, 116, 137–153.

KAMINER, H. & LAVIE, P. (1991) Sleep and dreaming in Holocaust survivors: Dramatic decrease in dream recall in well-adjusted survivors. *Journal of Nervous and Mental Diseases*, 179, 664–669.

KAUSHALL, P., ZETIN, M. & SQUIRE, L. (1981) A psychological study of chronic, circumscribed amnesia: Detailed report of a noted case. *Journal of Nervous and Mental Disorders*, 169, 383–389.

KEPPEL, G. & UNDERWOOD, B.J. (1962) Proactive inhibition in short-term retention of single items. *Journal of Verbal Learning and Verbal Behaviour*, 1, 153–161.

LEY, P. (1988) *Communicating with Patients: Improving Communication, Satisfaction and Compliance*. London: Chapman Hall.

LINDSAY, P.H. & NORMAN, D.A. (1977) *Human Information Processing: An Introduction to Psychology* (2nd edition). New York: Academic Press.

LLOYD, P., MAYES, A., MANSTEAD, A.S.R., MEUDELL, P.R. & WAGNER, H.L. (1984) *Introduction to Psychology – An Integrated Approach*. London: Fontana.

LOFTUS, E.F. (1975) Leading questions and the eyewitness report. *Cognitive Psychology*, 1, 560–572.

LOFTUS, E.F. (1979) Reactions to blatantly contradictory information. *Memory and Cognition*, 7, 368–374.

LOFTUS, E.F. (1997) Creating False Memories. *Scientific American*, September 50–55.

LOFTUS, E.F. & LOFTUS, G. (1980) On the permanence of stored information in the human brain. *American Psychologist*, 35, 409–420.

LOFTUS, E.F. & PALMER, J.C. (1974) Reconstruction of automobile destruction: An example of the interaction between language and memory. *Journal of Verbal Learning and Verbal Behaviour*, 13, 585–589.

LOFTUS, E.F. & ZANNI, G. (1975) Eyewitness testimony: The influence of wording on a question. *Bulletin of the Psychonomic Society* 5, 86–88.

LOFTUS, G. (1974) Reconstructing memory: The incredible eyewitness. *Psychology Today*, December, 116–119.

LUCE, T.S. (1974) Blacks, whites and yellows, they all look alike to me. *Psychology Today*, November, 105–6, 108.

LURIA, A.R. (1968) *The Mind of a Mnemonist*. New York: Basic Books.

MANDLER, G. (1967) Organisation and memory. In K.W. Spence & J.T. Spence (Eds) *The Psychology of Learning and Motivation*, Volume 1. New York: Academic Press.

McCLOSKEY, M. & ZARAGOZA, M. (1985) Misleading information and memory for events: Arguments and evidence against memory impairment hypothesis. *Journal of Experimental Psychology: General*, 114, 3–18.

McCORMICK, L.J. & MAYER, J.D. (1991) Mood-congruent recall and natural mood. Poster presented at the annual meeting of the New England Psychological Association, Portland, ME.

McILVEEN, R.J., LONG, M. & CURTIS, A. (1994) *Talking Points in Psychology*. London: Hodder & Stoughton.

MEMON, A. & VARTOUKIAN, R. (1996) The effect of repeated questioning on young children's eyewitness testimony. *British Journal of Psychology*, 87, 403–415.

MILLER, G.A. (1956) The magical number seven, plus or minus two: Some limits on our capacity for processing information. *Psychological Review*, 63, 81–97.

MILLER, G.A. & SELFRIDGE, J.A. (1950) Verbal context and the recall of meaningful material. *American Journal of Psychology*, 63, 176–185.

MORRIS, P.E. (1977) On the importance of acoustic encoding in short-term memory: The error of studying errors. *Bulletin of the British Psychological Society*, 30, 380.

MORRIS, P.E. (1992) Prospective memory: Remembering to do things. In M. Gruneberg & P.E. Morris (Eds) *Aspects of Memory*, Volume 1: *The Practical Aspects*. London: Routledge.

MORTON, J. (1970) A functional model for memory. In D.A. Norman (Ed.) *Models of Human Memory*. New York: Academic Press.

MURDOCK, B.B. (1962) The serial position effect in free recall. *Journal of Experimental Psychology*, 64, 482–488.

MURDOCK, B.B. & WALKER, K.D. (1969) Modality effects in free recall. *Journal of Verbal Learning and Verbal Behaviour*, 8, 665–676.

NEISSER, U. (1981) John Dean's memory: A case study. *Cognition*, 9, 1–22.

NEISSER, U. (1982) *Memory Observed*. San Francisco: Freeman.

NEISSER, U. & HARSCH, N. (1992) Phantom flashbulbs: False recollections of hearing news about Challenger. In E.O. Winograd & U. Neisser (Eds) *Affect and Accuracy in Recall: Studies of 'Flashbulb' Memories*. New York: Cambridge University Press.

PAIVIO, A. (1979) Psychological processes in the comprehension of metaphor. In A. ORTONY (Ed.) *Metaphor and Thought*. New York: Cambridge University Press.

PAIVIO, A. (1986) *Mental Representations: A Dual-Coding Approach*. Oxford: Oxford University Press.

PALMER, S., SCHREIBER, C. & FOX, C. (1991) Remembering the earthquake: 'Flashbulb' memory for experienced versus reproted events. Paper presented at the Annual Meeting of the Psychonomic Society, San Francisco.

PARKIN, A.J. (1987) *Memory and Amnesia: An Introduction*. Oxford: Blackwell.

PARKIN, A.J. (1993) *Memory: Phenomena, Experiment and Theory*. Oxford: Blackwell.

PENFIELD, W. (1969) Consciousness, memory and man's conditioned reflexes. In K. PRIBRAM (Ed.) *On the Biology of Learning*. New York: Harcourt, Brace Jovanovich.

PERIANI, D., BRESSI, S., CAPPA, S.F., VALLAR, G., ALBERONI, M., GRASSI, F., CALTAGIRONE, C., CIPLOTTI, L., FRANCESCHI, M., LENIZ, G.L. & FAZIO, F. (1993) Evidence of multiple memory systems in the human brain. *Brain*, 116, 903–919.

PETERSON, L.R. & PETERSON, M.J. (1959) Short-term retention of individual items. *Journal of Experimental Psychology*, 58, 193–198.

REBER, A.S. (1985) *The Penguin Dictionary of Psychology*. Harmondsworth: Penguin.

REDER, L.M. & ANDERSON, J.R. (1980) A comparison of texts and their summaries: Memorial consequences. *Journal of Verbal Learning and Verbal Behaviour*, 19, 121–134.

REEVES, A. & SPERLING, G. (1986) Attention gating in short-term retention of individual verbal items. *Psychological Review*, 93, 180–206.

REITMAN, J.S. (1974) Without surreptitious rehearsal, information in short-term memory decays. *Journal of Verbal Learning and Verbal Behaviour*, 13, 365–377.

RICHARDSON, J. (1993) The curious case of coins. *The Psychologist*, 6, 360–366.

RIPS, L.J., SHOBEN, E.H. & SMITH, E.E. (1973) Semantic distance and the verification of semantic relations. *Journal of Verbal Learning and Verbal Behaviour*, 12, 1–20.

ROY, D.F. (1991) Improving recall by eyewitnesses through the cognitive interview: Practical applications and implications for the police service. *The Psychologist*, 4, 398–400.

RUBIN, D.C. & OLSON, M.J. (1980) Recall of semantic domains. Memory and *Cognition*, 8, 354–366.

RUMELHART, D.E. (1975) Notes on a schema for stories. In D.G. Bobrow & A. Collins (Eds) *Representation and Understanding: Studies in Cognitive Science*. New York: Academic Press.

RUNDUS, D. & ATKINSON, R.C. (1970) Rehearsal procedures in free recall: A procedure for direct observation. *Journal of Verbal Learning and Verbal Behaviour*, 9, 99–105.

SALAME, P. & BADDELEY, A.D. (1982) Disruption of short-term memory by unattended speech: Implications for the structure of working memory. *Journal of Verbal Learning and Verbal Behaviour*, 21, 150–164.

SANDERS, G.S. (1984) Effects of context cues on eyewitness identification responses. *Journal of Applied Social Psychology*, 14, 386–397.

SCHANK, R.C. (1975) *Conceptual Information Processing*. Amsterdam: North-Holland.

SCHANK, R.C. (1982) *Dynamic Memory*. New York: Cambridge University Press.

SCHANK, R.C. & ABELSON, R.P. (1977) *Scripts, Plans, Goals and Understanding*. Hillsdale, NJ: Erlbaum.

SCHUMAN, H. & RIEGER, C. (1992) Collective memory and collective memories. In M.A. Conway, D.C. Rubin, H. Spinnler & W. Wagenaar (Eds) *Theoretical Perspectives on Autobiographical Memory*. Dordecht: Kluwer Academic Publishers.

SHALLICE, T. (1967) Paper presented at NATO symposium on short-term memory, Cambridge, England.

SHALLICE, T. & WARRINGTON, E.K. (1970) Independent functioning of verbal memory stores: A neurophysiological study. *Quarterly Journal of Experimental Psychology*, 22, 261–273.

SHULMAN, H.G. (1970) Encoding and retention of semantic and phonemic information in short-term memory. *Journal of Verbal Learning and Verbal Behaviour*, 9, 499–508.

SMITH, E.E., SHOBEN, E.J. & RIPS, L.J. (1974) Structure and process in semantic memory: A feature model of semantic decisions. *Psychological Review*, 81, 214–241.

SMITH, M.M., COLLINS, A.F., MORRIS, P.E. & LEVY, P. (1994) *Cognition in Action* (2nd edition). Hove: Erlbaum.

SMITH, S.M. (1979) Remembering in and out of context. *Journal of Experimental Psychology: Human Learning and Memory*, 5, 460–471.

SNOWMAN, J., KREBS, E.V. & LOCKHART, L. (1980) Improving information of recall from prose in high-risk students through Learning Strategy Training. *Journal of Instructional Psychology*, 7, 35–40.

SOLSO, R.L. (1995) *Cognitive Psychology* (4th edition). Boston: Allyn & Bacon.

SPERLING, G. (1960) The information available in brief visual presentation. *Psychological Monographs*, 74 (Whole No. 498).

SQUIRE, L.R. (1987) *Memory and Brain*. Oxford: Oxford University Press.

THOMAS, E.L. & ROBINSON, H.A. (1972) *Improving Reading in Every Class: A Sourcebook for Teachers*. Boston: Allyn & Bacon.

TULVING, E. (1968) Theoretical issues in free recall. In T.R. Dixon & D.L. Horton (Eds) *Verbal Behaviour and General Behaviour Theory*. Englewood Cliffs, NJ: Prentice-Hall.

TULVING, E. (1972) Episodic and semantic memory. In E. Tulving & W. Donaldson (Eds) *Organisation of Memory*. London: Academic Press.

TULVING, E. (1974) Cue-dependent forgetting. *American Scientist*, 62, 74–82.

TULVING, E. (1985) How many memory systems are there? *American Psychologist*, 40, 395–398.

TULVING, E. & PEARLSTONE, Z. (1966) Availability versus accessibility of information in memory for words. *Journal of Verbal Learning and Verbal Behaviour*, 5, 389–391.

TULVING, E. & THOMSON, D.M. (1973) Encoding specificity and retrieval processes in episodic memory. *Psychological Review*, 80, 352–373.

TVERSKY, A. & TUCHIN, M. (1989) A reconciliation of the evidence on eyewitness testimony: Comments on McCloskey and Zaragoza. *Journal of Experimental Psychology: General*, 118, 86–91.

VALENTINE, E.R. & WILDING, J.M. (1994) Memory expertise. *The Psychologist*, 7, 405–408.

WAUGH, N.C. & NORMAN, D.A. (1965) Primary memory. *Psychological Review*, 72, 89–104.

WELLS, G.L. (1993) What do we know about eyewitness identification? *American Psychologist*, 48, 553–571.

WICKENS, C.D. (1972) Characteristics of word encoding. In A. Melton & E. Martin (Eds) *Coding Processes in Human Memory*. Washington, DC: Winston.

WILDING, J.M. & VALENTINE, E.R. (1994) Memory champions. *British Journal of Psychology*, 85, 231–244.

WINGFIELD, A. (1979) *Human Learning and Memory*. New York: Harper & Row.

WOODWORTH, R.S. (1938) *Experimental Psychology*. New York: Holt.

WRIGHT, D.B. (1993) Recall of the Hillsborough disaster over time: Systematic biases of 'flashbulb' memories. *Applied Cognitive Psychology*, 7, 129–138.

WULF, F. (1922) Über die Veränderung von Vorstellungen. *Psychologisch Forschung*, 1, 333–373.

YESAVAGE, J.A. & ROSE, T.L. (1984) Semantic elaboration and the method of loci: A new trip for old learners. *Experimental Aging Research*, 10, 155–160.

YOUNG, C.V. (1971) *The Magic of a Mighty Memory*. West Nyack, NY: Parker Publishing Company.

YUILLE, J.C. & CUTSHALL, J.L. (1986) A case study of eyewitness memory of a crime. *Journal of Applied Psychology*, 71, 291–301.

INDEX